THE NEW
Coffeehouse
INVESTOR

HOW TO BUILD WEALTH, IGNORE WALL STREET, AND GET ON WITH YOUR LIFE

BILL SCHULTHEIS

PORTFOLIO

PORTFOLIO
Published by the Penguin Group
Penguin Group (USA) Inc., 375 Hudson Street, New York, New York 10014, U.S.A.
Penguin Group (Canada), 90 Eglinton Avenue East, Suite 700, Toronto, Ontario, Canada M4P 2Y3
(a division of Pearson Penguin Canada Inc.)
Penguin Books Ltd, 80 Strand, London WC2R 0RL, England
Penguin Ireland, 25 St. Stephen's Green, Dublin 2, Ireland (a division of Penguin Books Ltd)
Penguin Books Australia Ltd, 250 Camberwell Road, Camberwell, Victoria 3124, Australia
(a division of Pearson Australia Group Pty Ltd)
Penguin Books India Pvt Ltd, 11 Community Centre, Panchsheel Park, New Delhi - 110 017, India
Penguin Group (NZ), 67 Apollo Drive, Rosedale, North Shore 0632,
New Zealand (a division of Pearson New Zealand Ltd)
Penguin Books (South Africa) (Pty) Ltd, 24 Sturdee Avenue,
Rosebank, Johannesburg 2196, South Africa

Penguin Books Ltd, Registered Offices: 80 Strand, London WC2R 0RL, England

This edition published in 2009 by Portfolio, a member of Penguin Group (USA) Inc.

10   9   8   7   6   5   4   3   2   1

Originally published as *The Coffeehouse Investor*
by Longstreet Press (1998) and Palouse Press (2005).

Selections from Dalbar QAIB study used by permission of Dalbar, Inc.

Selections from *Morningstar Presentation Materials and Sales Ideas.*
Source: © 2008 Morningstar. All rights reserved. Used with permission.

Publisher's Note
This publication is designed to provide accurate and authoritative information in regard to the subject matter covered. It is sold with the understanding that the publisher is not engaged in rendering legal, accounting, or other professional services. If you require legal advice or other expert assistance, you should seek the services of a competent professional.

LIBRARY OF CONGRESS CATALOGING IN PUBLICATION DATA
Schultheis, Bill.
  The new coffeehouse investor : how to build wealth, ignore Wall Street, and get on with your life / Bill Schultheis.
      p. cm.
Includes bibliographical references and index.
  ISBN 978-1-59184-245-3
  1. Investments.   2. Portfolio management.   3. Finance, Personal.   I. Title.
  HG4521.S357825 2009
  332.6—dc22   2008036659

Printed in the United States of America
Set in Adobe Garamond

To all the Coffeehouse Investors,
Vanguard Diehards,
and everyone else who has taken a moment
to share this investment philosophy with others

CONTENTS

ON MARCH 8, 2000, TWO DAYS BEFORE THE NASDAQ STOCK index topped out at 5,048, I presented a Coffeehouse Investor seminar focusing on three simple principles that were introduced when this book was first published in 1998. These are lifelong principles that we all know to be true, principles that were probably shared with us long ago by a wise old friend.

1. **Don't put all your eggs in one basket.**
2. **There is no such thing as a free lunch.**
3. **Save for a rainy day.**

After the seminar, a middle-aged man named Bob approached me and admitted that he had connected with the three principles and needed to make some changes to his portfolio.

Bob had everything going for him. He revealed to me that he had just met the woman of his dreams and was preparing for a trip around the world. On top of that, he was set to retire and live happily ever after on a portfolio that had grown in value to over $1.6 million.

After meeting with Bob and reviewing his account, which consisted of something like twenty-five large-cap stocks and five mutual funds of the same flavor, we came to the conclusion that he didn't need to have much money at all invested in the stock market to maintain his lifestyle for the rest of his life.

After working with Bob to create a financial plan, I remember telling him, "It is time to diversify."

Intellectually he knew he needed to make some changes in his life, like buying some bonds, but emotionally he couldn't do it. How did I know that? Because four months later he called me and confessed he hadn't done a thing and his portfolio had plummeted about $500,000.

Again we reviewed his financial plan, and again I responded, "Bob, it isn't too late to diversify."

He nodded, but I knew he was thinking something different. . . .

"I own world-class companies."

"My stocks and mutual funds will come back, just like last time."
"My stockbroker is telling me to hang in there."
"My stockbroker's analysts are telling him to hang in there."
"I'll diversify when my portfolio gets back to $1.6 million."

Intellectually he knew he needed to make some changes, but emotionally he *still* couldn't do it. How did I know that? Because five months later he called me again and confessed he *still* hadn't done a thing and his portfolio had plunged another $400,000.

Again we reviewed his financial situation, and again I responded, "Bob, it still isn't too late to diversify."

He nodded again, but I knew he was thinking something different. . . .

"I own world-class companies."
"My stocks and mutual funds will come back, just like last time."
"My stockbroker is telling me to hang in there."
"My stockbroker's analysts are telling him to hang in there."
"I'll diversify when my portfolio gets back to $1 million."

The tragedy of this story is that instead of taking that trip around the world, Bob decided to go back to work.

Not because he wanted to.

Because he had to.

After thirteen years of working with retail and institutional accounts for a major Wall Street firm in Seattle, Washington, I decided to take a break. After stepping away from a career in the financial industry, it became obvious that an investment story very different from Wall Street's traditional story needed to be told. That is how this book came about.

Now, ten years later, after reflecting on the profound impact *The Coffeehouse Investor* has had on people's lives during a period of immense global turmoil and market volatility, it is time to reestablish these lifelong principles as fundamental to building wealth, ignoring Wall Street, and getting on with your life.

By choosing to read this book, you are taking a significant step toward creating a successful portfolio, which, for many of us, means building a nest egg to see us through our retirement years. No one said it was going to be easy; and right now there seem to be a lot more questions than answers about this thing called retirement, which means that this new chapter in your life can be full of predicaments or possibilities.

It all depends on you.

By choosing to read this book, you are also taking a significant step toward accepting personal responsibility for your retirement. That's good, because if we listen closely, corporations have been telling us for quite some time that we need to be more responsible for our retirement. On top of that, the government is starting to tell us that we need to be more responsible for our retirement.

The time to start is now.

Maybe one of the reasons this retirement thing is so daunting is because we are accepting responsibility for something completely opposite its definition. . . .

re•tire (rĭ-tīr'), v. **1.** to withdraw or go away to a place of privacy, shelter, or seclusion.[1]

I don't know about you, but that is *not* how I plan on spending my retirement. I want to live an abundant life every day for the rest of my life and have the financial resources to do it, and I'm sure you feel the same way.

The concept of retirement is still so new to our society,

because, for the most part, we are stepping away from our careers earlier and living longer. For example, in 1940 the average age of retirement was seventy, but the average life expectancy was only sixty-two. Today the average age for retirement is sixty-two, and the average life expectancy is seventy-seven![2]

Even though we are retiring earlier and living longer, our retirements shouldn't be about withdrawing or pulling away. These years should be about reaching out and expanding our possibilities of how we work and play, at a pace that reflects the energy level we have for both.

In visiting and working with countless investors who have properly prepared for retirement, I am inspired by the zeal that these people bring to this new chapter of their lives. It is a time for new friends, new discoveries, new passions, and new possibilities.

But I have also had too many discussions with too many people who carry with them a nervousness that they are going to outlive their money, and this nagging anxiety that they can't seem to shake saps the passion for life right out of their bones and right out of their lives. That is a tragedy because the goal, it seems to me, is to have our financial resources accentuate, not detract from, our capacity to live a full life for the rest of our lives.

Before we begin the journey of moving from predicaments to possibilities, let's take a look at how we got into this predicament in the first place.

In my opinion, the predicament took hold on August 16, 1982. I remember that day very well; in fact, I remember it as if it were yesterday. I was spending my summer vacation driving a wheat combine on the steep hillsides of our family farm.

I had just finished eating lunch on that hot summer day when the radio broadcaster announced that the Dow Jones Industrial Average had jumped thirty-nine points.

Holy Toledo, thirty-nine points.

You've got to remember, back in 1982, when the Dow was trading at 895, a ten-point swing in the market was a big deal. But that day the index surged thirty-nine points and stirred a sleeping bull. The stock market proceeded to generate an annualized return of 18.5 percent over the next eighteen years, which was about 80 percent more than its historical long-term average.

Holy Toledo.

I didn't know it then, but 1982 was also the year that a few corporations across the country began introducing self-directed retirement plans, better known as 401(k) accounts, into the workplace. Today these accounts are the primary retirement plan for millions of investors, but it wasn't always that way.

Once upon a time, if you were lucky enough to work for a corporation that offered one, you participated in its pension plan, otherwise known as a "defined benefit" plan. In this type of retirement plan, the corporation took on all the responsibility for saving enough money each year and investing it to meet its employee pension obligations. When you retired, the corporation sent you a monthly pension check for the rest of your life.

What a deal.

In the late 1970s and early 1980s, a few corporations started taking a closer look at specific sections of the Internal Revenue Code that, if interpreted correctly, allowed these same corporations to establish self-directed 401(k) accounts for employees and reduce the companies' commitments to their defined benefit pension plans.

You can probably guess what followed. Company after company began to adopt these 401(k) plans, and the result was a colossal shifting of responsibility for retirement saving off the backs of corporations and onto the backs of their own employees.

Yahoo! exclaimed the corporations, for obvious reasons.

Yahoo! exclaimed the workers, who began building 401(k) accounts in a stock market climate that was generating 18.5 percent annualized returns.

Yahoo! exclaimed Wall Street brokerage firms and mutual fund companies, who started charging outrageous fees to unsuspecting investors who were too busy living their lives to calculate the devastating impact that the outrageous fees would have on their long-term wealth.

Here's what happened next.

One by one, individual investors who were now responsible for saving enough money and investing it for retirement turned to the Wall Street crowd for a little guidance and came face to (smiling) face with an industry that was obsessed with people like Warren Buffett, Peter Lynch, and anyone else who "beat" the market with the accounts they managed.

In short, they encountered an industry that was obsessed with the pursuit of performance.

The financial industry tries to lure us into this pursuit of performance in many different ways, like touting its five-star mutual funds and number-one-rated stocks. Because of Wall Street's obsession with "beating the market," it is easy to succumb to this pursuit of performance. Eventually, we begin to think that the secret to building a successful portfolio is to "beat the market" with our stock market investments.

Unfortunately, the Wall Street crowd has never gotten around to telling us what to do when our five-star mutual funds and number-one-rated stocks underperform the market, only to be replaced with a new set of mutual funds and stocks the following year.

I guess we are supposed to figure that one out on our own.

As you may recall, the fun and excitement of buying and selling stocks and mutual funds came to a screeching halt in early 2000 when the Dow Jones Industrial Average topped out at 11,722, the NASDAQ index topped out at 5,048, and the S&P 500 index topped out at 1,527. For many investors, the party was over and the predicament had begun . . .

the predicament of saving enough money and investing it wisely to sustain yourself for what could conceivably be a ten- to thirty-year period of unemployment (called retirement).

If your goal is to embrace this thing called retirement with the same enthusiasm with which you are living your life today, the first step is to tune out the Wall Street crowd and tune in to yourself. This can be difficult, especially when you have been conditioned to follow Wall Street's pursuit of performance, which, for Bob, kept him from emotionally embracing three lifelong principles that he intellectually knew to be true.

After observing the habits of investors for a period that spans a career in the financial advisory arena, I have come to the conclusion that the greatest obstacle to building successful portfolios isn't finding five-star mutual funds and number-one-rated stocks; it is ourselves, and our reluctance to change and embrace the obvious. . . .

1. Don't put all your eggs in one basket.

The key to building a successful portfolio is to diversify your assets in such a way that you maximize your chances of reaching your financial goals with a minimum amount of risk.

2. There is no such thing as a free lunch.

Because markets are efficient, any attempt to beat the market is likely to prove disastrous to your long-term financial health. Thus, it is essential that you capture the entire return of each asset class, and leave it at that.

3. Save for a rainy day.

Developing a long-term financial plan, with a keen eye on your saving and spending levels, is essential for you to reach your long-term goals.

The benefit of diversifying in different asset classes such as stocks, bonds, cash, and real estate is that it allows you to achieve an appropriate level of risk within your portfolio, a level that is determined only after you first create your long-term financial plan. As Bob painfully discovered during the 2000–2002 bear market, depending upon your financial planning projections, it isn't worth it to take on additional risk in your portfolio if you don't need to.

The benefit of capturing the entire return of each asset class through low-cost index funds is that, in addition to the positive impact it will have on your financial wealth over the decades (quite possibly to the tune of hundreds of thousands of dollars, as we will find out in chapter 4), it is certain to have a profound influence on your emotional health as well.

Never again will you have to spend one ounce of energy on whether to buy or sell a particular stock or mutual fund based on its expected performance. Instead, your buy and sell decisions are methodically carried out on an infrequent basis for rebalancing purposes, according to the asset allocation targets you have established in your financial plan.

The benefit of developing a long-term financial plan is that, instead of focusing on five-star mutual funds and number-one-rated stocks, it allows you the opportunity to focus on questions that actually matter, like . . .

How much money should I be saving to reach my retirement goal?

When can I begin this new chapter of my life?

How much money can I withdraw each month during retirement?

Can I maintain my standard of living throughout retirement?

Am I prepared for unexpected medical expenses?

The three Coffeehouse Investor principles offer a sensible starting point for a young college graduate who is starting to contribute to a company-sponsored retirement account. All it takes is a commitment to save and an investment in one simple index fund to build wealth, ignore Wall Street, and get on with your life. Time is on your side.

On the other end of the spectrum, the three Coffeehouse Investor principles are even more important for anyone who is nearing retirement or is already living their retirement years. Taking on excessive risk at this point in your life without first creating a financial plan is a mistake you cannot afford to make, because time is not on your side.

For do-it-yourself investors, this book provides a foundation upon which you can build wealth, ignore Wall Street, and get on with your life.

If, however, you are someone who has a desire to work with a financial adviser, this decision can prove to be one of the best investments (or costliest mistakes) you will ever make. When choosing a financial adviser, make sure your adviser understands the profound impact the three Coffeehouse Investor principles will have on your financial and emotional well-being for the rest of your life.

It is one thing to have written a book almost a decade ago and called it *The Coffeehouse Investor*. It is another thing to go to work every day as a financial adviser and witness the significant impact these principles have had in real life with real people who need to make their financial resources last the rest of their lives.

Each passing year, I have noticed a significant increase in the number of investors who are tuning in to the Coffeehouse Investor philosophy. This has almost nothing to do with me and everything to do with people like you who connect with this philosophy and have a desire to introduce our three lifelong principles to family, friends, and coworkers. I invite you to do the same.

When we look around the world there is so much good work to be done, and it is a tragedy that so much mental energy is wasted trying to "beat the market." Working together to share the Coffeehouse Investor approach with others, we can have a profound impact on the lives of millions of investors who want to build financial *and* emotional wealth, ignore Wall Street, and get on with their lives. You can make a difference, as you already do.

The time to start is now.

1 THE COFFEEHOUSE INVESTOR

YOU ARE ABOUT TO EMBARK ON A JOURNEY THAT WILL change the way you invest forever. Along the way we will talk about things like pitching tents and pumpkin pies, because even though building and maintaining a successful investment portfolio today is essential for you to achieve your financial goals tomorrow, we will discover that the simple things in life, like pitching tents and pumpkin pies, are much more important to your investment success than the hype and hysteria of Wall Street, which never makes much sense anyway.

This journey is for everyone—longtime stock market investors as well as beginners, people who can't afford to make a mistake because their financial goals of tomorrow depend on making the right decisions today.

In our efforts to do the right thing with our investment decisions today, though, it's easy to get caught up in the empty words of Wall Street and do lots of wrong things. Well, if there is one place in your life where you don't want to make a mistake it is with your investment decisions, because when it comes to realizing your financial goal someday, if you make a mistake here, you won't get a second chance.

I must caution you, though: This investment journey will not show you how to pick hot funds and cool stocks, analyze balance sheets, predict business cycles, or forecast interest rates. This investment journey simply reveals the three principles of investing and explains why these principles are infinitely more important to your investment success than all the "stock market experts" who try to convince us they know more than we do about all this hot and cool stuff.

In fact, we will discover that one of the requirements for a successful journey is to ignore the "stock market experts" of today in much the same way Aristotle ignored the "flat world experts" 2,400 years ago when suggesting that the earth was round.

Oh, by the way, the last time I climbed Mount Rainier, I stopped just short of the 14,410-foot summit to drink some water and eat some food, and while hanging on to the side of the glacier at about five in the morning, I looked over my shoulder (briefly, because I suffer from acrophobia) and saw the sun . . .

rise . . .

and somewhere between Canada to the north and Oregon to the south, I think I detected a slight curve on the earth's horizon.

Now, I am not one to imply there is any correlation whatsoever between the flat-earth experts of yesterday and the stock market experts of today, but I will say, unequivocally, that stock market acrophobia, which is fueled in large part by stock market experts, causes many investors to make investment mistakes they are sure to regret when it comes time to retire.

Whether the earth is flat or round doesn't matter much anymore. What does matter is that most of us get up in the morning, put on our working shoes, and go to work,

> meeting deadlines,
> raising children,
> learning new technologies,
> building careers,
> attending school functions,
> keeping up with the competition,

and generally giving it all we've got.

For most of us, somewhere between the chaos of giving it all we've got today and achieving a financial goal tomorrow lies the daunting task of building and maintaining a successful investment portfolio.

It's hard enough putting a successful investment plan in place amid the chaos of giving all we've got every day. But when our efforts to do so come face to face with a financial industry that pretends to have all the right answers, there is a tendency to feel like we are slowly sliding off the side of a glacier.

As the world continues to gently spin 'round and 'round, as the days turn into nights and back into days again, our financial goals, which seem so far away, get closer and closer. The problem is, the world spins so gently, and we are so busy, that it's easy to put off dealing with faraway financial goals, especially when we have the misconception that dealing with something so far away means sorting through thousands of mutual funds, hundreds of stockbrokers, and dozens of financial magazines . . .

when all we really have the energy for is dealing with today.

That's why, with our lives so busy and our financial goals so far away, it's critical that, in addition to meeting deadlines, raising children, and keeping up with the competition, we learn about the three fundamental principles of investing. Once we do this, we can ignore Wall Street and get on with our lives, secure in the knowledge that by implementing the three fundamental principles of investing, our portfolios will be ready for us when we are ready for them.

Focusing on what really counts and ignoring everything else is a major step in any successful journey, because it is easy to get caught up in irrelevant things and follow along with the crowd. Then, even though you begin to notice that what you are doing is not getting you any closer to your goal, it is difficult to change your actions, especially when you see everyone else continuing to do the same thing.

For instance, one of my goals was to break eighty in golf. I practiced and practiced and practiced some more. I could not break eighty. Then one day I played golf with a woman twice my age and half my weight, who not only broke eighty, but shared with me the secret for doing so. After playing eighteen holes of golf on an old public course in West Seattle, she looked at me and said, "The problem with you is, you can't make your four-foot putts."

There is nothing like someone stating the obvious.

From then on, instead of going to the driving range to practice my driver, I went to the putting green to practice my four-foot putts.

Before long, I broke eighty.

Had I never run into that delightful woman, who cleared up my misconception that the secret to breaking eighty was hitting a perfect driver, I would still be practicing my driver and ignoring the most important thing of all—my four-foot putts.

It's not easy to go against the grain of popular opinion, especially when you show up at the putting green with your putter while everyone else is at the driving range, smacking their drivers. The same is true when building a successful portfolio—the challenge is to go against the grain of Wall Street by ignoring much of what they throw our way and focusing exclusively on the investment equivalent of four-foot putts . . .

or what I call the three principles of investing:

1. **Asset allocation**
2. **Approximate the stock market average**
3. **Saving**

Asset allocation means choosing the best combination of stocks, bonds, and cash to provide you with the greatest chance of achieving your financial goals with the least amount of risk.

Approximating the stock market average means making sure your stock market investments are doing at least as well as what the stock market as a whole is doing. (That is, if the stock market is up 2 percent, your stock market investments should be up 2 percent. If the stock market is up 33 percent, your stock market investments should be up 33 percent.)

Saving means knowing how much money you need to set aside each month to reach your financial goal and eventually saving it.

The important thing about asset allocation, approximating the stock market average, and saving is that these three principles are in our control. That is important, because we will see that when we focus on Wall Street, things that are out of our control, such as weekly economic numbers, quarterly earnings reports, and year-end mutual fund summaries, tempt us to fiddle around with our investments instead of leaving well enough alone.

Speaking of leaving well enough alone, I find it interesting that less than 10 percent of the millionaires of this country consider themselves "active" traders, and 42 percent of the millionaires of this country make less than one transaction per year in their investment portfolios.[1]

Not one transaction per hour,
not one transaction per day,

not one transaction per week,
not one transaction per month . . .

less than one transaction per year.

Maybe, just maybe, the millionaires of this country have
discovered that the more they leave well enough alone
and get on with their lives, pursuing their dreams and
fulfilling their passions, the better off they and their portfolios will be.

On the other hand, Wall Street types have a tendency to
portray this world of investing as fun, exciting, and full
of busy portfolios. To them, what could be better than
waking up each morning, logging on to the Internet after
reading the *Wall Street Journal,* then calling Stan the stockbroker and instructing him to buy a little of this and sell a
little of that, and please do it immediately because you
don't want to miss out on this great investment opportunity that is here today and gone tomorrow, and oh boy,

isn't this fun,
isn't this exciting,
isn't this luxurious . . .
and isn't life grand?

But for those of us who are greeted each morning with
children to be fed and dressed for school, and who are
completing projects for a ten o'clock seminar, running to

catch a bus, train, or automobile, and hoping for an extra three minutes to stop by the local coffeehouse for a cup of our favorite blend before dashing off to earn a living, spending time each day on our investments is the last thing we want to do.

I have never quite figured out how busy portfolios can somehow produce successful portfolios, but I have figured out that the secret to breaking eighty is making my four-foot putts.

As long as Wall Street has a vested interest in lots of transactions and busy portfolios, investors will continue to latch on to the hype and hysteria of Wall Street, perpetuating the misconception that by carefully reviewing market trends, diligently studying mutual fund tables, religiously researching global economies, and closely watching interest rates, anyone and everyone can successfully switch in and out of . . .

mid-cap health care funds,
emerging-market growth funds,
small-cap micro tech stocks,
and large-cap blue-chip funds . . .

and own a successful portfolio.

Hey! Wall Street now offers "mutual fund supermarkets," so investors can not only switch from fund to fund and stock to stock and sector to sector, they can now switch from one family of funds to another family of funds—

kind of like one-stop shopping.

And now Wall Street lets investors do all this one-stop shopping with the flick of a switch and the click of a mouse on the Internet.

How totally cool.

There's only one problem.

If the millionaires of this country aren't obsessed with trading their accounts every hour on the hour, who is?

You?

I have a good friend named Marilyn who is too busy juggling her activities as a great mother and successful attorney to design a sector-filled mutual fund account, but she still wants to own a successful portfolio for her retirement.

I have a good friend named Bernard who farms for a living and is too busy raising produce for supermarkets to come home at night and shop at a mutual fund supermarket, but he wants to own a successful portfolio for his retirement.

I have a good friend named Margaret who is a physical therapist and is too busy charting progress reports on her computer to trade stocks and mutual funds on the Internet, but she wants to own a successful portfolio for her retirement.

To these three people and millions like them who live life with a passion and purpose, and quite frankly couldn't care less about busy portfolios and all things Wall Street, congratulations—

you are on your way to becoming successful investors.

For those of us who already ignore Wall Street and are getting on with our lives, the challenge we face in building wealth is to spend a little time learning the difference (and what a difference it is) between busy portfolios and the three fundamental principles of investing.

It doesn't matter whether you have a regular (taxable) account and can choose between twenty thousand stocks and funds, or a company-sponsored 401(k) retirement plan that gives you a choice of eight. If you allocate your assets properly, approximate the stock market average, and save enough, you maximize your chances of achieving your financial goals.

It's a good idea to learn about these three fundamental principles of investing now, because the longer you wait the more painful it becomes, and the last thing you want to do is get caught in the middle of a growing national crisis resulting from too many people reaching retirement age with too little money to sustain themselves—not to mention enjoy themselves.

We've all read the surveys of the average baby boomer who has socked away exactly $26.32 and a few peanut butter sandwiches for her retirement. I suspect these surveys overstate the problem, but not by much.

If the people of this country who work so hard to earn a living continue with their current saving and investing habits, there will be lots of folks who are in for a big surprise when they want to retire, and this surprise won't come in the form of a surprise retirement party. It will come in the form of a dramatically reduced standard of living or a need to prolong their working years at a time in life when a peanut butter sandwich is the last thing they should have to worry about.

Do yourself a big favor. Put this book down, close your eyes, and contemplate what your life would be like, today, on 20 percent of your current income.

I would guess that for most people, living on 20 percent of their current income would be extremely painful, and if we're honest with ourselves we wouldn't begin to know where to cut and trim our expenses to match an 80 percent reduction in income.

If we slow our lives down just enough to determine whether there is a distant financial crisis looming, and then keep our lives slowed down a little longer to learn about the three fundamental principles of investing, it's a crisis that can easily be averted.

There is an enormous benefit to allocating your assets, approximating the stock market average, and saving.

It is the benefit of taking control of your financial life so that you, and you alone, are responsible for your actions today and the quality of life when you retire.

When you take control and accept full responsibility for how your assets are allocated, you are at the same time letting go of the mistaken belief that the secret to a successful portfolio is to accurately forecast bull and bear markets.

When you take control and accept full responsibility for approximating the stock market average, you are at the same time letting go of the mistaken belief that the secret to making money in the stock market is relying on stock market experts.

When you take control and accept full responsibility for how much you save, you are at the same time letting go of the mistaken belief that the government safety net will be there to catch you and millions like you when the time comes to retire in style.

A funny thing happens when you begin to take control of one part of your life—whether it is taking control physically, financially, or mentally: You gradually notice a positive change in other areas of your life, such as your personal relationships, your performance at work, and your ability to embrace your true passions.

Franz Schubert, the great Austrian composer, once said, "I am in this world only for composing."

Wouldn't it be nice to take some of our newfound energy and use it to discover or rediscover a sense of purpose in this world as strong as Franz Schubert's?

The first step in discovering our true passions and talents is to isolate and eliminate clutter in our lives, including in our finances, and a good place to start is to look at how our addiction to clutter is born out of the society we live in.

For instance, if a person is raised in a household that has a habit of watching television four hours a day, there's a good chance that person will become addicted to watching a lot of television.

I am not one to say four hours of television a day is too much television, but there is a little voice inside me that says four hours of television a day will not help me in my journey toward discovering my talents and passions and living a healthy and productive life. Unless people who watch four hours of television a day are creatively shown why watching that much television might be counter-productive to living healthy and productive lives, chances are these people will have a difficult time breaking their addiction to television.

Even though this addiction to television might hinder someone's ability to think creatively and communicate effectively, watching television is still a difficult habit to break, because for the most part those who are addicted probably don't know any better.

The same is true in investing.

If a person is raised in a society that has a habit of focusing on last year's top mutual funds, this year's hot stocks, and what the Dow Jones Industrial Average did today, eventually this person becomes addicted to the clutter of glossy mutual fund magazines, brokerage firms' recommended buy lists, and high-speed Internet sites, all proclaiming to have the right answers and top funds for you. Unless this person is creatively shown why paying attention to all this financial clutter is counterproductive to one's investment success, he will continue this addiction to Wall Street, all the while ignoring the three most important aspects of investing: asset allocation, approximating the stock market average, and saving.

It is a hard addiction to break, because after discussing the weather it seems like everyone wants to talk about cool companies and hot mutual funds, and if you don't own cool companies and hot mutual funds, some people might think you are dull and boring.

Don't worry.

It's better to be dull and boring and a successful investor than it is to be loud and obnoxious and unable to retire.

The ironic part of all this dull and boring stuff, if I do say so myself, is that the people who talk only about stocks and bonds are the people who end up being dull and boring. But the people who are embracing life and in their conversations reveal a sense of being immersed in the world at large are the people we enjoy the most.

Come to think of it, that's how this journey got started—meeting up with close friends at a corner coffeehouse in Seattle on rainy Saturday mornings, talking about the week behind us, talking about the week ahead, and talking about the kids to be coached, mountains to be climbed, and stuff to be done that day.

Those 6:30 A.M. coffeehouse discussions that helped us reconnect with the world after a hectic week usually got started around 6:45, when someone woke up enough to read something in the morning newspaper worth reading. It wasn't earthshaking news, but it was stuff we dealt with every day in our corner of the country, like how bad will traffic get before we finally pass a rapid-transit proposal? (it passed), or how will the Seattle Mariners' bull pen perform this year? (not great) . . . or how much higher (or lower) can Microsoft go?

The thing I liked most about those 6:30 Saturday morning coffeehouse discussions is that they were over and done with by 7:15, because by 7:15 it was light enough to see through the rain from our corner in the coffeehouse.

And even though we weren't that jazzed to leave our warm coffeehouse corner and go out in the rain to coach kids, climb mountains, or get stuff done, we got going anyway, because we learned early on that if you wait for a dry day to do stuff in Seattle it might just never get done.

Looking back on our discussions of soccer games and stock splits, those 6:30 A.M. coffeehouse investors seemed to be the independent type who enjoyed, among other things, the satisfaction of owning successful portfolios.

And even though they had fun talking about high-flying stock market issues, these investors understood the importance of diversification, and they also knew that when you take a risk in the stock market, you better make sure it is a risk worth taking.

Abraham de Moivre, the French-born mathematician and pioneer in the understanding and application of risk management, never sat with us at our corner coffeehouse table because he died in 1754, but to me he is the ultimate coffeehouse investor. He used to spend his afternoons in an English coffeehouse, selling his knowledge of risk to gamblers, merchants, and brokers.

I'm convinced that, were he alive today, Abraham de Moivre would tell us that while investing at least a portion of our money in the stock market to achieve our long-term financial goals is clearly a risk worth taking . . .

relying on Wall Street experts to invest our money in the stock market for us is clearly a risk that is not.

Don't take my word for it, though.

This journey will let you decide for yourself.

Let's get going.

2 THIS THING CALLED RISK

ONE KEY TO BUILDING A SUCCESSFUL INVESTMENT portfolio is to eliminate the risk you can control and reduce the risk you can't.

One key to living life with a passion and a purpose is to say yes to personal risks you can control and embrace the risks you can't.

In looking at ways we can reduce or eliminate this thing called investment risk, let's begin by attempting the impossible, which makes for an exciting journey because it's not very often one gets a chance to attempt the impossible.

I wonder what Sir Edmund Hillary and Tenzing Norgay felt like standing on top of Mount Everest.

I wonder what Roger Bannister felt like running the first sub-four-minute mile.

I wonder what my mother felt like getting eight children ready for early church on Sunday mornings.

If you've never had a chance to attempt the impossible, your wait is over and your time is now. We are about to attempt the impossible feat of taking a very simple subject—asset allocation—and keeping it simple amid a financial industry that has a knack for making the subject of asset allocation sound very complicated, very technical, very confusing, and very much out of the grasp of anyone who might just happen to possess a little common sense of her own—

which,
I'm assuming,
you do.

Asset allocation simply means dividing up your assets in the right proportions among stocks, bonds, and cash to maximize your chance of achieving your financial goal with the minimum amount of investment risk. Unfortunately, keeping the subject of asset allocation simple is easier said than done, because Wall Street has mastered the art of talking out of both sides of its mouth.

I think you know what I mean.

On one side of its mouth, Wall Street whispers about the merits of long-term investing. On the other side of its mouth, Wall Street appeals to our sense of fear and greed by talking about short-term stock market volatility and short-term mutual fund performance.

Just for the heck of it, stand in front of a mirror sometime and try talking out of both sides of your mouth as successfully as the financial industry does. It's not that easy to do.

The problem with Wall Street talking out of both sides of its mouth is that many investors who are tuned in to their own lives and consumed with their own careers are not quite sure what side to listen to—and often end up listening to the side that talks about daily stock market swings and irrelevant mutual fund things.

But then, what can you expect?

That's the loudest side.

It's the side that wants to discuss how your assets should be allocated among capital appreciation funds, blue-chip growth stocks, high-yield bond funds, balanced Latin American utility funds, mid-cap tech stocks, short-term microchip government funds, growth and income balanced funds, emerging market small-cap stocks, large-cap equity funds, and medium-term, mortgage-backed, reverse-repo sector funds.

And it should come as no surprise to us that the loudest side is also the side that happens to appeal to our emotions of fear and greed. It isn't easy to keep the subject of asset allocation simple in the midst of a financial industry that tends to appeal to our fear and greed. After all, we don't want to lose money in the stock market (fear). Nor, if we already have a good deal, do we want to miss out on a better deal (greed).

And in an effort to get your business and the fees and expenses that go along with your business, the financial industry can't resist moving from a discussion of long-term investment strategies to conversations about instant account access, next quarter's earnings estimates, online hookups, bear markets, standard deviations, daily switching privileges, ten-day moving average trend lines, hourly portfolio valuations, cool Web sites, sector fund rotations, and all the other stuff that encourages you to switch the account, send them the money, make the transaction, and lock in the fee (meaning *their* fee).

Let's keep in mind that we live in a country where the bottom line is number one, and the financial industry certainly isn't the only industry that is prone to a little fast talking to do what it has to do to make the boss happy.

There are lots of good things that come out of a country that focuses on the bottom line, like a willingness to get the job done because if you don't somebody else will. We need to remember one thing, though. When living in a country in which the bottom line is number one, we are ultimately responsible for our own actions, and if your effort to allocate your assets turns into lots of trades and transactions and your portfolio suffers as a result, you can only blame that person in the mirror.

So let's take responsibility for our own actions and simplify the subject of asset allocation.

Again, asset allocation simply means dividing up your assets in the right proportions among stocks, bonds, and cash to maximize your chance of achieving your financial goal with the minimum amount of risk.

The critical first step in allocating your assets is to determine what is known as your investment time horizon; that is, the years you have left to invest before you start drawing on your investments (which, for most of us, means retirement), and then using your investment time horizon to figure out how to divide up your assets in the right proportions among stocks, bonds, and cash.

For example, a twenty-five-year-old with a long investment time horizon needs to make sure that the majority of his assets (80 percent to 100 percent) are invested in common stocks, which are riskier than bonds or cash in the short term but prove better investments in the long term. On the other end of the spectrum, a sixty-four-year-old retiree should consider investing a significant part of her assets (50 percent to 90 percent) in bonds and/or cash in order to reduce the impact of inevitable stock market declines and to supplement income for living expenses.

How should you allocate your assets? When deciding on the proper mix among asset classes, it is important to remember there is no perfect answer. The objective in allocating your assets is to allocate them so your portfolio broadly represents where you are in relation to your investment time horizon.

The sample portfolios in the following charts are simple guidelines to use when allocating your assets among stocks, bonds, and cash, using a retirement age of sixty-five as a yardstick for your investment time horizon.

As you can see, even in the most conservative investment portfolio a portion of assets should still be allocated to the stock market to protect the investor from the debilitating impact of inflation.

At the end of each year, review the amount of money you have invested in each class of assets. If a substantial movement in the stock or bond market results in a significant

ASSET ALLOCATION MODELS

Age	Conservative		Aggressive	
20–45	Cash	10%	Cash	0%
	Bonds	20%	Bonds	0%
	Stocks	70%	Stocks	100%
46–60	Cash	10%	Cash	5%
	Bonds	40%	Bonds	15%
	Stocks	50%	Stocks	80%
60+	Cash	10%	Cash	10%
	Bonds	70%	Bonds	30%
	Stocks	20%	Stocks	60%

shift away from your desired allocation, you should consider rebalancing your assets to your original allocation percentages, unless, of course you feel comfortable with your current allocation. The following table gives an example of reallocating assets among classes.

ORIGINAL ALLOCATION $200,000	70% in stocks	$140,000
	25% in bonds	$50,000
	5% in cash	$10,000
AFTER TWO YEARS $240,400	STOCKS ARE UP 30% TO	$182,000
	BONDS ARE DOWN 5% TO	$47,500
	CASH IS UP 9% TO	$10,900
	RESULTING BALANCE	$240,400
INVESTOR REBALANCES $240,400 TO ORIGINAL ALLOCATION	70% IN STOCKS	$168,280
	25% IN BONDS	$60,100
	5% IN CASH	$12,020

Understanding this thing called risk and how it applies to you when allocating your assets is very important, because when it comes to making long-term investment decisions, many of us have a tendency to confuse investment risk with investment opportunity; and we end up allocating too much of our money to investments that are counterproductive to reaching our financial goals based on our investment time horizon.

The first step in understanding this thing called investment risk is to define it—not in the way Wall Street defines it, which makes no sense at all—

$$\sigma = \sqrt{\frac{1}{n-1} \cdot \sum_{t=1}^{N} (r_t - \bar{r})^2}$$

but in a way that makes sense in a real world, full of real people doing real jobs and paying for real things, such as college educations, new automobiles, and new homes: *Investment risk is the risk that the money you are counting on to purchase something important or sustain your lifestyle at some point in the future won't be there when you need it.*

There are two major types of investment risk. The first type is inflation—the risk of having your living expenses increase faster than the income generated from your investments.

The second type of risk is stock market volatility—the risk of losing money in the stock market.

Wall Street doesn't talk much about the first type of risk, inflation, but it does talk a lot about the second type of risk, stock market volatility. Of course. That's the risk that generates lots of trades and transactions.

If we were to take a very scientific survey and call up ten thousand stockbrokers, mutual fund managers, and financial analysts and ask them about the risks of investing, I have a sneaking suspicion their perception of investment risk would look something like this . . .

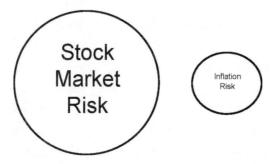

And because the financial industry looks at risk this way, there is a natural tendency for us to look at risk this way.

Instead of looking at investment risk the way Wall Street does, let's look at investment risk based on our investment time horizon.

The chart on page 29 shows the yearly fluctuations of the stock market from 1926 to 2007. As you can see, if you had an investment time horizon of one year or less, there was about a 30 percent chance your stock market money would go down in value during this time period.

Obviously, if you have a one-year investment time horizon and your money is invested in the stock market, you need to weigh the risk of keeping it in the stock market against the importance of having 100 percent of your principal intact one year from now.

The next chart shows five-year stock market returns from the same time period. As you can see, when you increase your investment time horizon from one year to five years, your chance of losing money in the stock market drops dramatically.

The final chart shows ten-year stock market returns. As you can see, for investors with a time horizon of ten years or longer (which includes most of us), the risk of losing money in the stock market is reduced yet again.

That is not to say there will never be a ten-year period in which you will lose money in the stock market. In fact, during any ten-year period there is a strong probability you will endure a two- or three-year period in which your stock market investments will decline 20 percent,

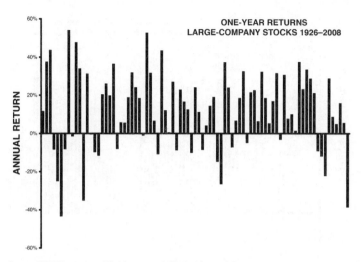

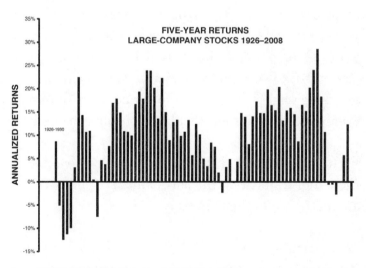

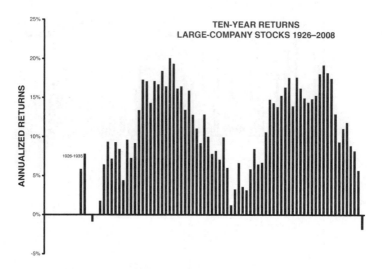

30 percent, or more. That's the stock market for you. But as you can see, when you have an investment time horizon of ten years or more, an investment in the stock market is clearly a risk worth taking—even if you do have to wait a few more years for the market to bounce back from the inevitable declines in value that happen from time to time.

Even so, I suspect there might be a few investors out there (not to mention the entire financial industry), who are muttering to themselves,

Hey, wait a minute!
Ten years is a long time to stick with something,
especially when I am having trouble
making it through the week,

*and every time I turn on the TV or read the newspaper
or talk to my neighbor it seems like the Dow
is having a cow.*

For those investors with a ten-year investment time horizon who are having trouble making it through a one-week, Wall Street–induced investment time horizon, you might want to make a copy of the ten-year stock market chart and tape it to your bedroom closet door, so that the next time the Dow has a cow you can keep things in perspective and remain committed to your long-term investment strategy.

Because, while Wall Street talks about Dows that have cows, a very unobtrusive word—inflation—continues to eat away at our purchasing power in subtle, subdued ways that quietly blend in with our daily activities of paying for groceries, paying for health care, paying for tuition, paying for automobiles, and paying for everything else that goes up in price in amounts too small to merit any attention on the nightly business report when the Dow has a cow and drops five hundred points.

And while Wall Street is frantically running around screaming, "Get a doctor, get a doctor, the Dow is having a cow!"

One year in college has gone from $1,245 to $13,200.

An automobile has gone from $5,817 to $28,400.

A one-day hospital stay has gone from $173 to $1480.

A home has gone from $39,400 to $298,600.

The price of a stamp has gone from four cents to forty-two cents

(and last I heard they were thinking forty-four cents).[1]

Maybe those of us who have a ten-year investment time horizon (or longer) and live in the real world of college educations, automobiles, homes, and 42-cent postage stamps should call up those ten thousand Wall Streeters and tell them this is how we view investment risk. . . .

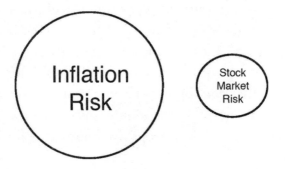

On second thought, don't waste your time.

The easiest way to focus on your long-term investment time horizon and ignore the short-term Wall Street stuff is to ignore the short-term Wall Street stuff.

We all know that the stock market is volatile in the short run because most of us monitor it in the short run. And I am the first to admit that when you follow the stock market on a daily or weekly basis it can be a little nerve-racking, as indicated by the graph below, which shows the movement of the stock market during a three-month period in 1997. This three-month period, if I do say so myself, has an eerie resemblance to a risky mountain-climbing expedition, encouraging even the bravest of long-term investors to stay at home and hide (their money) under a mattress.

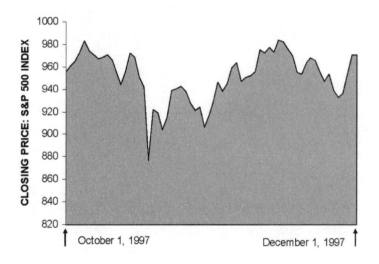

Now compare our risky mountain-climbing chart to the graph below, which simply reflects the long-term (logarithmic) growth of a $1,000 investment from 1926 to 2007.

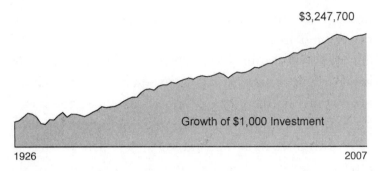

$3,247,700

Growth of $1,000 Investment

1926   2007

With so many things going on in our lives, we sometimes lose sight of the fact that the three-month period indicated by the risky mountain-climbing chart is the same three-month period that appears as a mere point on the chart of the market's long-term performance.

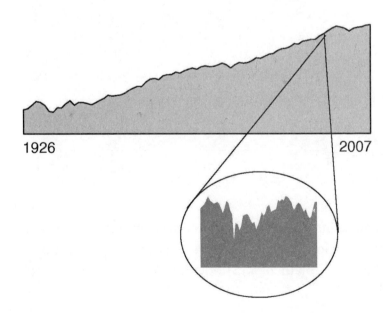

1926   2007

The graph you focus on plays a big part in how you view risk and allocate your assets. Let's face it, if you are addicted to daily stock market swings, there will be times when the short-term volatility in the stock market will make you feel like you are caught hanging on the side of a cliff, and you will be inclined to do things with your investments that are not so smart, like switch mutual funds, trade stocks, or move to the sidelines. In reality, the smartest thing you can do is direct all your attention to your family, your career, and your pursuits, bolstered by an inner confidence that your stock market investments are invested in the chart that doesn't resemble a risky mountain-climbing expedition.

I'm not saying this is an easy task to accomplish, because the financial industry is obsessed with talking about economic avalanches and financial crevasses much more than the price of a postage stamp—and it is only human nature to fear avalanches and crevasses much more than a four-, er, forty-two-cent stamp.

For long-term investors who monitor their portfolios four times a year instead of every day, not only is it easier to keep their assets properly allocated, thus minimizing the investment risk that affects them the most—inflation—but doing so frees up more of their creative energy to maximize the personal risks that enrich them the most. Before long, they realize that the personal risks they want to take in life are not that risky. They are an adventure.

The first time I climbed Mount Rainier was a miserable experience. I climbed with someone who talked too much. I rented my climbing boots and they wore a red hole in my foot. I borrowed a backpack and the strap broke. The stove wouldn't light. It rained.

But we made it to the top.

Looking back on the times I have summitted Mount Rainier since then (and I have failed many more times than I've succeeded), my favorite ascent was with a man and a woman who were traveling across America one summer after graduating from a college in Virginia— having a good time and sleeping in the back of their truck, stopping in state after state to hike and climb. (Hey, it's great to be young.)

For some crazy reason, our climbing party and the two students from Virginia met halfway up Rainier.

Two of them and two of us.

There's not much happening halfway up Rainier, but that's where the crevasses start and that's where summer-time hikes turn serious, requiring those who want to continue on to get out . . .

their crampons,
seat harnesses,
ice axes,
carabineers, helmets,
ice screws,
pickets, and ropes.

The two from Virginia had everything except a rope, so we invited them to clip onto our rope and climb with us. You know, the more the merrier.

When climbing Rainier, there is one spot you don't want to dillydally around—the spot on Ingraham Glacier at 11,500 feet that needs to be crossed to get to Disappointment Cleaver—because big blocks of ice have been known to come hurtling down the middle of Ingraham Glacier, causing massive avalanches. And so dillydally we didn't.

At 12,000 feet our two friends from Virginia wanted to turn around. At 13,000 feet they wanted to turn around. At 13,500 feet they wanted to turn around. At 13,501 feet they wanted to turn around. At 14,410 feet we all wanted to turn around—and we did, because we had made it to the top.

Going up Rainier is the easy part, because in the middle of the night the glacier is frozen. The footing is firm, and the hot sun hasn't come up yet. Going down is a different story. The sun is hot, you are tired, and the glacier is slushy, forcing you to knock slushy snow off your sticky crampons every step of the way. (Clumps of snow on the bottoms of your feet are not quite as effective as clean crampons when jumping over a crevasse.)

And when you cross Ingraham Glacier on the way down, things can get a little dicey, because the chunks of ice that have been known to come hurtling down the mountain have now had a couple of hours to melt and break free. Fortunately, on this day, the falling chunks of ice were a few minutes early, but not so early that we weren't able to witness an enormous avalanche in front of our eyes.

I suspect the four of us individually reflect on that avalanche from time to time, though I'm not sure because I've never kept in touch with those two students from Virginia.

Not everyone climbs mountains.

Everyone does encounter risk, though, along with the emotional avalanches that are a part of failing and succeeding amid this thing called life.

Whether it's the risk of presenting a new idea at work in the heat of battle to keep up with the competition, or the risk of recognizing you need to get away from it all and just chill out at your favorite coffeehouse, you only live life once, and you can't let a few emotional avalanches now and then keep you from embracing your dream in pursuit of your summit.

I used to chop thistles on our farm with a kid who, when a plane flew over, would look up, wipe his sweaty brow, and dream out loud of becoming an airline pilot. As I remember, this simple event of chopping thistles, wiping sweaty brows, and dreaming out loud happened several times a day for several years during the hot months of August on a wheat farm in eastern Washington.

This kid did not know the difference between a rudder and a stabilizer, but he did know, in fact he was absolutely positive, he'd rather be piloting an airplane than chopping thistles.

Somewhere today there is an airplane crisscrossing this country copiloted by my kid brother, who works for a major airline; and sometimes I wonder what he is dreaming about today.

The journey continues.

3 APPROXIMATING THE STOCK MARKET AVERAGE

THE PRODUCTIVITY AND GROWTH OF OUR COUNTRY is simply a reflection of all the brilliant, ingenious, commonsense ideas that are put into action through lots of hard work by you, your friends, and your neighbors.

And unless I'm missing something, it seems to me that when we take our hard-earned money and invest it in the stock market, what we are really doing, consciously or unconsciously, is making a commitment to this collective creativity of human beings based on the premise that this unending flow of ideas, combined with our innate desire to improve the quality of life of ourselves and others, will not stop anytime soon.

Unfortunately, Wall Street takes this very simple and very successful approach to investing and screws it up by trying to convince us that the secret to our investment success lies in breaking up this collective creativity to invest in specific stocks, industries, trends, and mutual funds instead of investing in everything.

It would be one thing if Wall Street were successful in its efforts to beat the entire stock market average by investing in specific stocks, industries, trends, and mutual funds. But when Wall Streets efforts to selectively pick and choose continually underperform this collective creativity (as reflected by the entire stock market average) and end up costing you hundreds of thousands of dollars in the process, that's where we need to draw the line.

Maybe we should start from square one.

As you probably know, the annual return of the stock market average is a collective return of all the publicly traded companies listed on a particular index, such as the Standard & Poor's 500 index or the Wilshire 5000 Index. The good companies as well as the not-so-good companies. Logically, you would think that stock-picking "experts," as mutual fund managers claim to be, who spend all day analyzing financial reports, interviewing company presidents, talking to research analysts, reading the *Wall Street Journal,* and generally feeling important and intelligent, could pick enough good companies and avoid enough bad companies to outperform the stock market average, which is made up of all the good companies and all the bad companies combined.

They can't.

They don't.

This is Wall Street's best-kept secret, and it's a secret mutual fund managers would rather you didn't know.

It's kind of like hiding a bad report card from your parents.

Now you know.

Only 27 percent of all managed mutual funds beat the stock market average during the last fifteen-year period.

Only 55 percent of all managed mutual funds beat the stock market average during the last ten-year period.

Only 36 percent of all managed mutual funds beat the stock market average during the last three-year period.

Only 14 percent of all managed mutual funds beat the stock market average in each of the last three-, ten-, and fifteen-year periods.[1]

Amazingly, these report cards would be significantly worse if the following statistics were included:

- the expenses paid on load mutual funds
- the capital gains tax liability of mutual funds held in taxable accounts
- merged or discontinued funds

If I were a mutual fund manager, I'd want to keep this a secret too.

I've had a few bad report cards in my life, including the one I got from Sister Lucida after telling her that I didn't get much out of her religion class. But I have to say, in my eight years of attending Guardian Angel School, I never had a report card quite as ugly as the report cards of mutual fund managers.

If these report cards were handed out by Sister Lucida, I suspect most mutual fund managers would be stuck in eighth grade.

Investors who decide to invest their hard-earned money with these underperforming stock-picking experts are destined to underperform the stock market average with them.

It's that simple—and this costly.

The following table shows how much underperforming the stock market average costs someone who invests $500 a month over a thirty-year period.

	UNDERPERFORMING BY THIS AMOUNT		
YEARS	2%	3%	4%
5	$ 2,567	$ 3,545	$ 4,491
10	$ 16,561	$ 21,597	$ 26,294
15	$ 52,837	$ 67,604	$ 80,873
20	$ 129,966	$ 164,459	$ 194,266
25	$ 280,572	$ 351,856	$ 411,026
30	$ 561,363	$ 697,977	$ 806,752

(assuming yearly stock market return of 10%)

Not surprisingly, mutual fund managers go to great lengths to hide these bad report cards by drawing our attention away from them and directing it toward performance numbers that have nothing to do with our long-term investment success:

I'M NUMBER ONE!
(for the last three weeks)

I'M NUMBER ONE!
(for risk-adjusted, large-cap mutual funds that begin with the letter *x*)

I'M NUMBER ONE!
(for Euro-Pacific biotechnology cat food funds)

I'M NUMBER ONE!
(at missing four-foot putts)

Unfortunately, as the report cards reveal, there aren't too many mutual funds that are number one at consistently beating the stock market average.

This phenomenon of underperformance by mutual fund managers is difficult for many investors to accept because many of us have come to depend on experts in many areas of our lives, including our stock market investments, and the thought that professional stock pickers could collectively do such a lousy job is hard for many investors to comprehend.

For instance, Dale, my dentist, is an expert at taking care of my teeth.

Greg, my mechanic, is an expert at taking care of my car.

Fred, my doctor, is an expert at keeping me healthy.

In a society that finds comfort in experts, it is only natural to want a "stock-picking expert" to pick stocks for us, because investing is a very serious thing, especially when the quality of our retirement depends on it.

I can assure you, if Dale, my dentist, Greg, my mechanic, or Fred, my doctor, had a report card as bad as mutual fund managers' I would be in the market for a new dentist, mechanic, and doctor; and so would you.

With all due respect to mutual fund managers, who try their hardest and do a very good job at hiding bad report cards, I know of no other industry in which so many self-proclaimed experts try so hard to convince us that they are wildly successful at that at which they so miserably fail—outperforming the stock market average.

The problem is that Wall Street is so successful at drawing our attention away from bad report cards that most investors have come to accept this mediocrity, oblivious to any alternatives.

Guess what. *There is an alternative.*

Most of you have probably heard of it by now: approximating the stock market average; that is, coming as close to equaling it as possible.

One way to do this is to invest in a stock index mutual fund. As many of you already know, a stock index fund is simply an unmanaged mutual fund that owns a piece of all the companies of a particular stock market index. The good companies and the not-so-good companies combined.

What a brilliant, ingenious, commonsense idea—which I can't take credit for but can religiously pass along to those of you who want to unclutter your financial lives and own a sophisticated portfolio. And boy, wouldn't Sister Lucida be proud of me for finally doing something a little religious.

Before we go further, let's discuss the difference between stocks and mutual funds. (It never hurts to review what you probably already know, so here we go.)

When you invest in a common stock, you become part owner in that company. When you invest in a mutual fund, you indirectly own common stock in many companies. These stocks are all bundled together in one investment called a mutual fund. Managed mutual funds have a person or group of people who call themselves mutual fund managers. Mutual fund managers spend all day trying to make sense out of interest rates, predict future earnings growth, look for undervalued companies, and predict overvalued situations, and they do all this with the goal of providing their investors with a rate of return that is better than a specific stock market index.

At least I hope that's their goal.

A stock index fund is also a mutual fund, but an unmanaged mutual fund. Because it owns a piece of all the publicly traded companies that make up a particular stock market index, there is no need for any kind of manager to decide what stocks the fund should invest in. Pretty nifty, eh?

History has shown that an investment in the collective creativity of human beings, as represented by a piece of all the publicly traded companies in an unmanaged stock index mutual fund, is much more profitable over time than an investment with a mutual fund manager who tries to "beat" the stock market average, even though mutual fund managers try with all their might to convince us otherwise.

I suppose that with Wall Street saying "I'm number one" in your ear every day of the year, it is only natural for you to think that the secret to being a successful investor is to beat the stock market average with your stock market investments. But by trying to beat the stock market average it is easy for investors to ignore the fact that the stock market average itself has historically provided an excellent investment, and by trying to beat an already good thing you are virtually guaranteed to *end up below it.*

When building and maintaining an investment portfolio, the first step in breaking this addiction to mutual fund managers is to understand why these stock pickers consistently underperform the stock market average. The first reason mutual fund managers consistently underperform the stock market average is that the stock market is already very efficient. In other words, because there are millions and millions of investors out there, if there is a good deal to be had, more often than not somebody has already grabbed it.

For example, if someone scatters seven thousand-dollar bills next to the Empire State Building, would you call your travel agent and book a flight to New York in the hopes of retrieving a thousand-dollar bill?

I doubt it.

Why not?

You wouldn't waste your time and money because you would logically conclude that somebody would beat you to the seven thousand-dollar bills. In picking stocks, as with finding thousand-dollar bills, once in a while there is a lucky person, but with millions of stock pickers out there, most of the time someone will have beaten a mutual fund manager—or you—to that next underpriced stock.

(For those of you who are caught up in the world of Wall Street things and think it is possible for mutual fund managers to consistently find underpriced stocks in a marketplace filled with millions of investors, and think that the example of the thousand-dollar bill at the Empire State Building is a little silly, the 86 percent of fund managers who were unable to beat the stock market average in each of the last three-, ten-, and fifteen-year periods have done a wonderful job of proving my point.)

The second reason why mutual fund managers consistently underperform the stock market average is that the money they manage is subject to extremely high annual expenses, which reduce your total return.

Quite simply, a $350 plane ticket to New York is too much to pay on the off chance you may find a thousand-dollar bill.

Mutual fund expenses, buried deep in the middle of every mutual fund prospectus, may seem like a few cents here and a few cents there. Unfortunately, these expenses end up costing investors (yes, even smaller investors) hundreds of thousand of dollars over time, as we will find out in chapter 7. Managed mutual funds have a vested interest in keeping Wall Street's best-kept secret a secret by trying to convince us that picking the good stocks and avoiding the bad stocks is a sophisticated science better left in the hands of a stock market expert.

Nothing could be further from the truth.

Even so, I have found that many investors are a little wary at first when introduced to this brilliant, ingenious, commonsense concept of investing in the entire stock market average as represented by an unmanaged stock index mutual fund. Maybe we should see whether there are any other investors out there who embrace this unconventional approach of investing in the entire stock market instead of specific stocks, industries, trends, and mutual funds.

Let's check in with some of the largest and most sophisticated investors in our country—the administrators of state pension funds. These people invest billions of dollars and have a fiduciary responsibility to do the right thing for the thousands of state employees who are counting on their state's pension fund when they retire. First we'll call my home state of Washington and find out how much of its stock market money is indexed in the collective creativity of our country.

What? 100 percent?

No. No. No.

We don't want to know the chance of rain in Seattle on the Fourth of July. We want to know how much of the state pension fund's domestic stock market money is indexed to approximate the stock market average.

100 percent?

No kidding?

Let's check in with the state of California. What? You index 85 percent?

Okay; I admit, out here in the Wild West we tend to be a little off the wall. Let's head east and see what other state pension funds are doing.

Kentucky? What? You index 67 percent of your portfolio?

Florida? What? You index 60 percent of your portfolio?

New York? What? You index 75 percent of your portfolio?

Connecticut? What? You index 84 percent of your portfolio?[2]

Hmm. When talking with state administrators, my favorite response was from the administrator of a very large state pension fund of a state that shall remain anonymous (though we Mariner baseball fans don't much care for the pinstriped uniforms of one of its baseball teams), who said that for long-term investors, "not only is it unreasonable to think they can beat the stock market average, it's probably not doable."

To be honest with you, I can't quite picture the administrator of a state's public pension portfolio going home at night, stopping at the grocery store to pick up some eggs, milk, and fruit, and then casually throwing into his shopping basket the latest mutual fund magazine from the magazine rack to browse through after dinner in the hopes of picking up a few hot mutual fund ideas for his state's pension fund.

But what the heck, let's say he did.

In February 1994, one of the top mutual fund magazines ran this cover story: "Where to Make Money in '94— The Best Funds to Buy!" and listed the top eight domestic stock mutual funds to own. Four years later, each of these eight mutual funds had underperformed the stock market average, and collectively they underperformed it by an average of 25 percent annually.

If a state administrator stuck my retirement money in a mutual fund portfolio that underperformed the stock market average by 25 percent annually, I would call him immediately and politely ask him to switch his after-dinner magazine reading material to *National Geographic.* This is advice our common stock portfolio can do without, unless of course you have an uncontrollable urge to underperform the stock market average by 25 percent annually.

Unfortunately, that's how many individual investors make their investment decisions—looking for mutual funds that tout good track records, because track records would seem to be the most logical way to choose a fund, even though it has been shown again and again that past mutual fund performance has little to do with future mutual fund performance. In fact, using past performance numbers as a method for choosing mutual funds is such a lousy idea that mutual fund companies are required by law to tell you it is a lousy idea by listing the following disclaimer in their prospectuses:

Past performance is no indication of future performance.

Maybe investors are attracted to past performance numbers because past performance numbers work so well when selecting things like dishwashers.

When it comes our turn to buy a dishwasher, do we go to the appliance store, plunk down a chunk of change, blindly point to a dishwasher in the corner, and say, "I'll take that lonely one over there"? No. We do a little research, like maybe asking our friends and neighbors which ones they've liked, and then combine that information with research from something like *Consumer Reports* to find out which dishwasher has performed best in the past, and then buy it.

Unfortunately, there is one small problem with using the dishwasher method to select mutual funds.

It doesn't work.

And investors who continue to use the dishwasher method of selecting mutual funds based on past performance numbers are destined to be washing dishes when it comes time to retire.

History has shown it is not such a good idea to invest in mutual funds that have a track record of outperforming the stock market average.

The following ten-year track records suggest you are better off investing at a horse track than in a mutual fund that has at one time or another been a top dog (horse?).

The top twenty-five mutual funds from 1988 to 1998 dropped on average to 1,851 out of 3,021 funds during the next ten years, collectively underperforming the stock market average during the later period.

Mutual funds in the top quartile from 1988 to 1998 collectively underperformed that period's bottom quartile during the next ten-year period.[3]

With track records like the ones above, how should an investor choose a superior mutual fund? You might be surprised at how easy your choice is. Let's play a quick game called "Outfox the Box."

You are the contestant. There are ten boxes. Each box has some money in it, from $1,000 to $10,000, and you know much is in each box. You get to choose a box, and these are your choices:

$1,000	$2,000	$3,000	$4,000	$5,000
$6,000	$7,000	$8,000	$9,000	$10,000

(Remember, you know how much is in each box.)

Drumroll, please . . .

The crowd is screaming.

Your heart is pounding.

Which one will you choose?

This is not a trick question. The answer is obvious. Anyone would choose the $10,000 box. Your decision to choose a mutual fund is just as easy. This time we will change the rules a little. This time, we are going to hide the amounts in the boxes. Except for one box. For this box we reveal that it contains $8,000.

The choices look like this.

$8,000	?	?	?	?
?	?	?	?	?

Now, which box will you choose?

This answer is also obvious.

You would choose the $8,000 box, because the chance of increasing your winnings is just not worth the risk of choosing an amount substantially less—unless, of course, you are a gambler.

This is not a book on gambling.

This is a book on investing.

There is a big difference.

With the stock market average consistently outperforming 75 percent to 85 percent of all managed mutual funds, it is a tribute to the massive marketing machine of Wall Street that so many investors spend so much time and effort trying to select the top mutual funds instead of following the lead of state pension fund administrators who have a vested interest in choosing the $8,000 box instead of gambling.

It's important to keep this silly little game in mind when dealing with Wall Street, because Wall Street loves to criticize the concept of indexing as a boring approach to investing in which you forego all opportunity to beat the stock market.

What Wall Street is really saying is,

"Ignore the $8,000 box and give us your money and we will gladly choose another box for you, because we are the self-proclaimed experts at 'outfoxing the box,' and even though the odds are long and the chances are slim that we will succeed, let's give it a try because we love you and your fees."

Sometimes it takes a silly little game called "Outfox the Box" to break this addiction of always trying to beat the stock market average. It is a hard addiction to break, because the concept of having a superior mutual fund by investing in a mutual fund that reflects the stock market average is a difficult concept to grasp, especially when thousands of mutual fund managers and thousands of investment advisers and glossy mutual fund magazines are telling you that investing in the stock market average is a mediocre approach to investing in the stock market. Indexing is a case of average being superior, and at first it seems illogical, but, in reality, it's not illogical at all. It's simply common sense.

I frequently encounter this addiction to trying to "Outfox the Box" in friends and investors who tell me they have switched mutual funds several times in the last few years and are still searching for a top-notch mutual fund.

First, I explain to my friends the concept of indexing, which means investing in the entire stock market.

Second, I point out that most mutual funds underperform the stock market average over time.

Next, we review why track records are meaningless when trying to choose a top mutual fund, because the top mutual funds of today tend to underperform the stock market average in the future. And finally, we play a silly little game called "Outfox the Box."

However, most investors are so addicted to relying on past performance numbers, not to mention stock market experts, that I have to start all over.

First, I explain to my friends the concept of indexing, which means investing in the entire stock market.

Second, I point out that most mutual funds underperform the stock market average over time.

Next, we review why track records are meaningless when trying to choose a top mutual fund, because the top mutual funds of today tend to underperform the stock market average in the future. And finally, we play a silly little game called "Outfox the Box."

My favorite response was from a friend of mine who is an environmental scientist and restores parks in San Francisco. For many years, she had been switching from fund to fund, searching for funds that were best for her. One day she called me, looking for a consistent long-term mutual fund for her portfolio.

First, I explained to her the concept of indexing, which means investing in the entire stock market. Second, I pointed out that most mutual funds underperform the stock market average over time. Next, we reviewed why track records are meaningless when trying to choose a top mutual fund, because the top funds of today tend to underperform the stock market average in the future.

Her response to me was, "I know you like those index funds, but besides that, what is a good fund to invest in?"

So we started all over.

First, I explained to her the concept of indexing, which means investing in the entire stock market. Second, I pointed out that most mutual funds underperform the stock market average over time. Next, we reviewed why track records are meaningless when trying to choose a top mutual fund, because the top funds of today tend to underperform the stock market average in the future, and finally we played a game of "Outfox the Box."

Suddenly, a lightbulb went on. Her exact reply to me was, "Why would anyone consider anything but indexing?"

At that moment, my friend from San Francisco freed herself from the clutter of Wall Street, which is a big load off her shoulders because she is one person who would rather spend her time restoring parks in San Francisco than sorting through fifteen thousand mutual funds and seven thousand stocks every other year in an effort to build and maintain her common-stock portfolio.

Oh, by the way, I hope you enjoy the parks the next time you are in San Francisco.

4 BUILDING A COMMON-STOCK PORTFOLIO

ONCE YOU REMOVE YOURSELF FROM WALL STREET'S complete and total obsession with trying to beat the stock market average and accept the fact that approximating the stock market average is a rather sophisticated approach to the whole thing, building a successful common-stock portfolio becomes an immensely gratifying experience.

Especially when you relax and remember that you are building a common-stock portfolio, not a space shuttle.

This is important, because even though we all have that innate creativity that yearns to build something and watch it grow—whether it be a project at work, a child, or a garden—we also have a tendency to throw up our hands in despair and call in the experts when faced with a task that those same experts have labeled "too compli-cated for you."

Building a common-stock portfolio can be summed up in one word: diversify, diversify, diversify.

Okay, three words.

Diversification simply means making sure your stock market investments are aligned with the collective cre-ativity of our country and are not subject to the more volatile ups and downs of specific stocks, industries, trends, or business cycles. That's not to say fortunes haven't been made in one-stock portfolios, because they have. Just ask Bill. No, not me.

The other Bill.

It is probably very exciting to have your entire portfolio invested in one stock that goes up and up forever, al-though I wouldn't know because it has never happened to me. But the rewards of owning a one-stock portfolio need to be weighed against the risk of having that same one-stock portfolio go down and down forever as you approach retirement.

The more your portfolio is diversified in many different companies in many different industries, the less your fi-nancial goal is dependent on your or anyone else's ability to successfully pick individual stocks, industries, or trends—something mutual fund managers have proven is not easily done.

That's why indexing your portfolio makes so much sense. Not only does it give you the ultimate in diversification by owning the widest selection of companies in the maximum number of industries, but it simplifies your selection process of narrowing down fifteen thousand funds and seven thousand stocks to a couple of sensible mutual funds.

The simplest approach to diversifying your stock market investments is to invest in one index fund that represents the entire stock market. The problem with having your entire common stock portfolio invested in one "entire stock market" index fund is that eventually, at some backyard barbecue, you will cross paths with a Wall Streeter who, upon learning that your entire portfolio consists of only one mutual fund, will argue that you are way underdiversified and will pay for that mistake the next time the stock market drops.

Just smile and say, "Please pass the potato salad."

HOWEVER . . . even though an entire-stock-market index fund is a simple, smart way to invest—especially for those who currently have twelve different mutual funds and eight different stock positions and no earthly idea how these investments are performing, much less how they all fit together—we can combine this thing called diversification with our index-fund approach and divide our stock holdings among three groups:

large company stocks,
small company stocks,
and international stocks

and build a common-stock portfolio using three index funds that represent each of these three groups of common stocks.

The advantage to investing in three separate index funds instead of one entire-stock-market index fund is that it takes this diversification thing one step further by introducing other dimensions of the market into your portfolio that move dissimilarly to large company stocks in the short run, if not the long run. And it allows you to construct a personalized portfolio to match your temperament and investment time horizon.

For instance, investors who have a longer time horizon and are able emotionally to accept increased volatility can add to their holdings in small-cap stocks and thus provide themselves with an opportunity for increased returns over time beyond what large-company stocks offer. But for investors with a more conservative demeanor, or those who are nearing a financial goal, owning more large-company stocks should be considered, as these stocks have traditionally been less volatile than small-company stocks and have provided more income from dividends.

The following illustrates two portfolio approaches to diversifying among three groups of index funds.

AGGRESSIVE PORTFOLIO

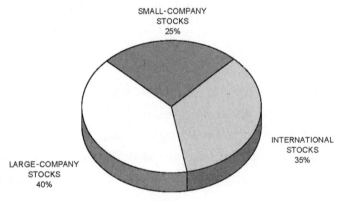

SMALL-COMPANY
STOCKS
25%

INTERNATIONAL
STOCKS
35%

LARGE-COMPANY
STOCKS
40%

CONSERVATIVE PORTFOLIO

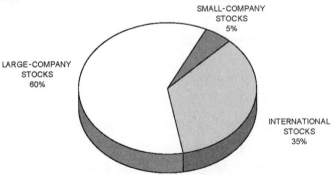

SMALL-COMPANY
STOCKS
5%

LARGE-COMPANY
STOCKS
60%

INTERNATIONAL
STOCKS
35%

In addition to choosing a three-index-fund approach, you can take this thing called diversification one step further by adding three more dimensions of the market to your portfolio—value, small value, and REITS (real estate investment trusts)—and build an indexed portfolio utilizing these different dimensions of the market. Instead of owning three index funds, your common-stock portfolio would now consist of six index funds:

large-company,
large-company value,
small-company,
small-company value,
international,
and REITS.

Keep in mind that if you choose to add value and growth index funds to your portfolio, you are doing nothing more than fine-tuning an already good thing. It simply takes this thing we're talking about—diversification—one (small) step further. (For help in selecting index funds among these five groups, turn to the appendix, which lists index funds by categories.)

In chapter 2 we learned the importance of annually re-balancing your investment portfolio among stocks, bonds, and cash to make sure your investments are in line with the type (and amount) of investment risk you want to maintain. The same rebalancing concept holds true for the common-stock portion of your portfolio. Whether the common-stock portion of your portfolio is aggressive or conservative, the most important factor when diversifying is to adhere to this asset allocation strategy, because when you stick to your strategy and rebalance your assets at year-end, buy and sell decisions are no longer arbitrary but are instead objectively carried out according to your predetermined plan. The result: a portfolio that has less volatility without sacrificing performance.

Let's look at an example of rebalancing a common-stock portfolio at year-end with an investor who makes an initial investment of $40,000.

ORIGINAL ALLOCATION: $40,000	60% LARGE-COMPANY INDEX FUND	$24,000
	25% SMALL-COMPANY INDEX FUND	$10,000
	15% INTERNATIONAL INDEX FUND	$6,000
AFTER ONE YEAR: $43,400	LARGE COMPANIES ARE UP 12% TO . . .	$26,880
	SMALL COMPANIES ARE UP 7% TO . . .	$10,700
	INTERNATIONALS ARE DOWN 3% TO . . .	$5,820
	RESULTING IN A YEAR-END TOTAL OF . . .	$43,400
AT WHICH TIME THE INVESTOR REBALANCES THE YEAR-END TOTAL TO HER ORIGINAL ALLOCATION	60% OF $43,400 IN LARGE-CO. FUND	$26,040
	25% OF $43,400 IN SMALL-CO. FUND	$10,850
	15% OF $43,400 IN INT'L FUND	$6,510

Sometimes it is emotionally difficult to reallocate assets away from the class that is doing well (in this case, large-company stocks) and invest them in the class that has underperformed. But those who neglect this important aspect of portfolio diversification often find that when the tide eventually turns (as it always does), they are stuck with an excessively large, underperforming asset class.

It's easy to rebalance a portfolio in a tax-deferred retirement account because you are not subject to a capital gains tax on profits taken. This means you can sell stock as part of your rebalancing plan and not have to pay taxes on any profits from that sale—those profits are reinvested within your tax-deferred account.

If instead you have a regular (taxable) account, you need to consider the impact a capital gains tax will have on your rebalancing efforts. In this case, instead of selling and buying to rebalance your account as we did in the above example (again, because selling stock in a taxable account might result in capital gains taxes), it might make sense to leave existing money where it is and direct new money into that portion of your portfolio that is underrepresented according to your desired allocation strategy. Before you make any portfolio changes that could result in a significant tax liability, it's always best to consult with your accountant or tax attorney.

The task of building an indexed common stock portfolio is pretty straightforward. Unfortunately, many qualified retirement plans, including 401(k)s, still do not include index funds. For those investors whose only investment in common stocks is through retirement plans that do not include index funds, choices are not as simple.

In my opinion, any company that doesn't provide employees an opportunity to invest in index funds should be held accountable to its employees to the extent that the company plan's managed mutual funds underperform their respective stock market indices.

Plan A for solving this problem is to go to your employers and encourage them to include index funds in their choice of funds (which most companies already do). If they balk, politely ask whether they would be willing to make up the difference to the extent that the managed mutual funds underperform their respective benchmark indices.

If Plan A fails or if you hesitate to share a little common sense with your employer, try Plan B: Anonymously give your employer a copy of this book and highlight this chapter.

If your employer thinks indexing a retirement account is a far-fetched idea, tell your employer that indexing is the

preferred method of investing for the very large and sophisticated public pension plans that have a fiduciary responsibility to do the right thing in providing for their
employees at retirement, and you are wondering whether
they have the same type of commitment.

If Plan A fails and Plan B fails, try Plan C:
Make lemonade out of lemons.

That is, continue to focus on the goal of approximating
the stock market average with the managed mutual funds
you have chosen from your company plan by not switching them, trading them, or swapping them for something
else—except when you rebalance your investment portfolio every year-end.

If you need help figuring out which of your plan's
funds fall into which categories (large-cap, small-cap,
and international), ask your benefits coordinator or
mutual fund company to help you. If you find out that
your retirement plan has ten large-company funds, six
small-company funds, and four international funds, it
is not necessary to own all twenty funds. Choose one
or two from each group and then stick with them. If
your funds begin to underperform the other funds in
the same group, don't worry about it, because once you
switch to another fund, you have fallen into the trap of
using the dishwasher method of choosing mutual

funds, which we found out in the last chapter doesn't work.

Remember, if you invest in more than two actively managed mutual funds in each of the three common-stock groups, you are making your investment journey unnecessarily cluttered.

Diversification and making sure you come as close as you can to approximating the stock market average are what building a common-stock portfolio is all about. Unfortunately, the ease with which you are able to access your account through tools such as telephone switching privileges or access through the Internet might lead you to believe that your stock market success is based on your ability to quickly and cleverly move among top funds and hot stocks and navigate through an uncertain economy.

This switch to the get-rich mentality that is so pervasive in the investment world is absolutely disastrous for someone who is serious about building and maintaining a successful common-stock portfolio.

What I just said is so important to your investment success I will repeat it.

This switch to the get-rich mentality that is so pervasive in the investment world is absolutely disastrous for someone who is serious about building and maintaining a successful common stock portfolio.

We're not quite finished.

In addition to investing in mutual funds in a qualified retirement account, many employees who work for publicly traded companies are also given the opportunity to invest some of their retirement money in company stock. If you think you are working for a good company, then it is a good idea to own some of that company. But be careful. Too much of a good thing can turn out to be a bad thing.

I know, because I like ice cream.

There are countless instances in which great companies have experienced declines of 40 percent, 50 percent, 60 percent, or more in the price of their stock for no explainable reason, even when the stock market as a whole has gone up in value. If you feel confident in your ability to predict the inexplicable and are willing to risk a substantial amount of your retirement assets on this ability, then who am I to caution otherwise?

If you prefer a successful, diversified investment strategy instead with the money you are counting on to live on when you retire, don't allocate more than 10 percent to 20 percent of your retirement money to your company's common stock, and don't forget to reallocate your company stock in the same way you reallocate your other assets at the end of each year.

Enough said.

Let's talk about food—my favorite subject.

5 MY FAVORITE PIECE OF PIE

I CAN'T WAIT TO TALK ABOUT FOOD, BECAUSE IF YOU ask me, using your creative energies in the kitchen is a lot more fun (and productive) than trying to figure out which way the stock market is headed. And wouldn't you know it, the more time you spend on fun and productive things (like baking pies, my specialty), the less time you spend worrying about hot stocks and cool mutual funds.

This is important, because if you are a long-term investor and you are constantly worrying about hot stocks and mutual funds, you are ignoring the biggest piece of the investment pie—*compounding*—and it is a piece of the pie you can't afford to ignore.

From 1978 to 2007, a $10,000 investment in the stock market average would have grown, with dividends reinvested, to $386,140. Of that $376,140 increase, 40 percent was due to the price of the underlying common stocks going up in price, and 60 percent was due to the reinvestment of dividends.[1]

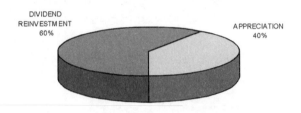

IMPACT OF DIVIDEND REINVESTMENT
S&P 500 INDEX 1978–2007

DIVIDEND
REINVESTMENT
60%

APPRECIATION
40%

A little background: Most companies pay out some of their profits each quarter to their shareholders—a dividend. Recipients have the option of taking this dividend check, cashing it and spending it, or reinvesting it—that is, buying *more* shares of a particular stock or mutual fund. This is called dividend reinvestment.

When we reinvest our dividends instead of spending them, we are able to earn dividends on our original dividends. Ideally, we turn around and reinvest those dividends in order to earn even more dividends. All this stuff of earning dividends off dividends off dividends off dividends is called compounding. Most companies increase their dividends each year, so, as an added bonus, the money you compound is constantly increasing.

Albert Einstein, a pretty bright guy, once said something to the effect that "the eighth wonder of the world is the powerful effect that compounding has on your money."

I shared this largest-piece-of-pie story once with a friend of mine who replied, "Yeah, but the smallest piece of the pie is where all the action's at." So, for everyone interested in "action," you can skip the rest of this chapter. But for those who want to build wealth, ignore Wall Street and get on with your lives, you might find the subject of compounding compelling, even though it means letting your investments just sit there and compound

and compound

and compound.

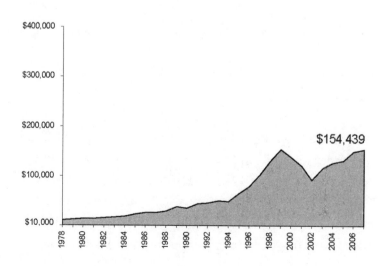

Let's look at this from a different angle.[2]

The previous graph shows how a $10,000 investment in the stock market grew over a twenty-year period when the investor took all the dividends in cash. The graph below shows how this same $10,000 investment grew when the dividends were reinvested.

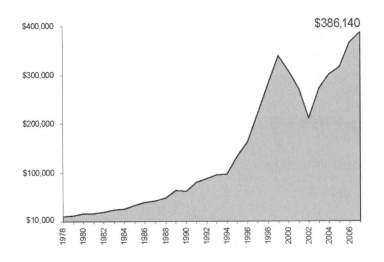

Big difference, huh?

The nice thing about owning a stock index mutual fund, or any other mutual fund for that matter, is that you can elect to have all of your dividends automatically reinvested.

Investors who spend time selling stocks and mutual funds that go up in price are missing out on the largest piece of the money pie because they don't give their investments a chance to sit there and do what they are supposed to do—compound. If you own stocks or mutual funds and reinvest the dividends, your money is put to work in the biggest piece of pie, and the time you save by not obsessing over buy-low and sell-high strategies can be used to pursue those things in your life you really have fun at . . .

like baking pies.

Speaking of pies, people who bake pies have a blood pressure level one third lower than that of society at large.

According to me.

When you bake a pie, you can't help but smile and feel in harmony with the world. My favorite pie is pumpkin pie. It tastes great and is less filling. You know you're off to a good start when you read the ingredients in a can of pumpkin pie mix:

pumpkin.

No monosodium glutamate.

No thiamine mononitrate.

No sodium tripolysphosphate.

No potassium phosphate.

Just pumpkin.

Here's all the stuff you need:

1 16-ounce can solid-pack pumpkin
1 egg
1 cup sugar
1 teaspoon cinnamon
1 teaspoon pumpkin pie spice
1 12-ounce can evaporated milk
1 9-inch pie shell

Preheat the oven to 425°F. Dump all the above stuff (except the pie shell) into a bowl and stir it up, and then dump all the stirred-up stuff into the pie shell and stick it in the oven. (Please note: If you use a metal pie dish, bake the pie with a cookie sheet underneath so the bottom of the pie shell doesn't burn.) After fifteen minutes, reduce the heat to 350°F. Bake for about forty or fifty minutes. Stick a knife in it, and if it comes out clean, you're done.

You can now show your friends and family the powerful impact that dividend reinvestment has on your very own pumpkin pie!

I love this pie stuff, but we must be moving on.

6 SAVING IT

WRITING A CHAPTER ON SAVING IS NOT MY IDEA OF A
good time.

It would be much more fun to talk about the intricacies
of pitching a tent at 14,500 feet on a windy day on the
side of the tallest mountain in North America, Mount
McKinley (or Denali, for you geography buffs) in Alaska.
It is kind of like trying to read the newspaper on the
hood of your car while traveling down the freeway at
sixty miles per hour in a snowstorm.

Pitching a tent in a snowstorm with the wind blowing at
sixty miles per hour is a lot like life: Sometimes you have
to make a conscious decision to have fun, because if you
don't, it quickly becomes the most miserable experience of
your life. In fact, I have taken this concept of consciously

deciding to have fun and applied it to other areas of my life, like running out of gas on the freeway, attending the office Christmas party, or running the last three miles of a marathon, and I have to say it works pretty well.

The second decision when pitching a tent during a sixty-mile-per-hour snowstorm is a decision to postpone pitching the tent unless the wind calms down or a snow wall is built up. All it takes is one lost tent to decide that this is a smart decision.

After a snow wall is built and the tent is pitched and the temperature hits thirty-five below zero, it's a great feeling to climb inside a sleeping bag that is warrantied to keep you warm for another five degrees.

If there is one thing that is more exciting than building a snow wall and pitching a tent and crawling into a warrantied forty-below sleeping bag in thirty-five-below weather, it's doing all these things and then realizing . . . you have to go.

When it is thirty-five below and you have to go, you go

outside . . .

and go, and then quickly go back inside.

The problem is, you can't go by the tents because if everybody went by the tents there wouldn't be any clean white snow left to melt on the stove the next morning for coffee. When you are hundreds of miles away from the nearest coffeehouse and it is blowing cold and thirty-five below, you'd best not mess with anyone's coffee. So, every year, a designated go place is established about a hundred yards from the tents of the 14,500-foot base camp, causing records to be set all night long in the Denali Invitational hundred-yard dash.

Or so it seems.

The real fun though, on Denali, is not building snow walls or pitching tents or forty-below warm sleeping bags or hundred-yard dashes. The real fun is getting to 14,500 feet. Fun, that is, if you enjoy carrying a sixty-pound pack and dragging a fifty-pound sled uphill, in the snow and cold, for seven days and twelve miles.

As I recall, the first day was not much fun. Not because of the heavy load. Not because the brutal cold combined with unbearable heat (when the clouds disappeared) made life miserable. The first day was not much fun because of the silence and aloneness.

Silence and aloneness as stark as the white Alaska wilderness.

Silence and aloneness.

During the next few days of nothing but cold, silence, and the empty feeling of aloneness, I finally realized I was losing my balance. Not the tip-toe-gingerly-around-a-bottomless-crevasse type of balance, but the back-home-in-Seattle type of balance between family, career, and especially myself amid the clutter of everyday life.

Discussions, disagreements, deadlines, traffic, television, telephones—and you know the rest.

After living this routine for many years, I realized on a cold, desolate mountain, somewhere in the middle of nowhere, I was addicted to the clutter of everyday life, and it finally dawned on me that the clutter in my life might be keeping me from pursuing my dreams and living a life I would choose to live if given a chance to do it all over again.

This left me with two options:

Remove some clutter and strike a balance, or pray that someday I would get a second chance.

It's easy to strike a balance on Denali—the balance of sitting tight in a blinding snowstorm and moving higher when the weather breaks, in search of a goal called the summit. The real challenge we face is to strike a balance in the valleys of our everyday lives, because it's in the valleys—not on some desolate mountain—that we pursue our dreams, live our lives, and make things happen.

When you get right down to it, removing a little clutter in the process of striking a balance is exactly what saving and spending is all about.

All this important investment stuff, like asset allocation, indexing, diversification, tax deferral, compounding, keeping score, rebalancing, and living life, doesn't do a whole lot of good if we can't strike a balance between saving and spending.

I think you know what I mean.

Now, it might seem like I am oversimplifying the obvious by focusing on saving as an important component to building wealth, ignoring Wall Street, and getting on with our lives, but as we begin to think about this subject I think you will agree with me that the emotional complexity of saving, combined with the magnitude of its importance, is something many of us need to look at and evaluate.

It seems to me that when it comes to building and maintaining our investment portfolios amid the chaos that swirls around us, it's easy to bypass the inward responsibility of saving and focus instead on investment things that are out of our control, like daily stock market quotes, quarterly earnings reports, and year-end mutual fund summaries, because looking at issues outside of us is a lot easier than dealing with issues inside of us, like our saving and spending habits.

In short, it's much more fun to do a midyear portfolio review than it is to do a midyear personal review.

Striking a balance between saving and spending starts with making a conscious decision to take a step back from the countless activities that consume your every waking moment long enough to calculate approximately how much you should save each month to reach a financial goal. This is something most investors don't do. According to a recent *Wall Street Journal*/NBC News poll, 57 percent of investors have not spent any time calculating how much money they should be saving to reach a retirement goal.

That's quite a few people who are driving in the dark without headlights, hoping to arrive safe and sound at a destination called retirement.

In talking about how much you should save, I am not going to suggest that you radically change your lifestyle, because I know you won't. After all, the lifestyle you are living today is probably the result of myriad decisions made over time, including new jobs, new homes, new cars, new relationships, new children, new neighborhoods, new recreational pursuits, and new dreams.

What's more important than a sudden, radical lifestyle change is being fully aware of the gap between how much you are currently saving and how much you *should* be saving to reach your goal, so that when financial decisions come up in the future, such as buying a new this or a new that, the issue of being responsible for your financial future is at least present at your financial decision-making table.

Then, if the decision to buy a new this or a new that is made today, it is made in an environment in which you are fully responsible for your actions and are able to give yourself full credit for who you are and the decisions you make. The pleasure and satisfaction we derive from being fully responsible for our decisions, and the quiet confidence that comes from knowing those decisions are the right ones, is infinitely more gratifying than the uncertainty of not knowing the implications of our decisions.

The first rule in doing a personal review in order to strike a balance between saving and spending is to do the review in the context of the world we live in, not the world Wall Street lives in. Because Wall Street—and Madison Avenue—are very fond of portraying this retirement thing as gray-haired grandpas and grandmas bicycling through the backroads of France and walking hand in hand on exclusive resort island beaches.

Uh, excuse me.

Having millions and millions of dollars at retirement would be nice, but let's face it, not everyone is going to vacation in the south of France and fly first class the rest of their lives. Some retirees might prefer to do something else.

Keep in mind that the millions and millions of dollars Wall Street says you need at retirement are numbers created by an industry that has a habit of paying out yearly bonuses of millions and millions of dollars to individual employees. Somewhere along the line Wall Street has forgotten that we can retire and be happy on a little less than millions and millions of dollars.

The problem with using multimillion-dollar retirement figures to compute our savings target today is that this amount can overwhelm us to the point that we are either frozen by inaction or begin to save so rigorously that we miss out on the pleasures of today.

That's why it's important to strike a balance.

Listen: It is not worth making your life miserable today so you can retire in style tomorrow.

Let's face it, most of us are not going to change our lifestyle to the point where we are able to save what Wall
Street says we need to save to be happy and enjoy life. I
mean, who wants to forego a family vacation next summer, and all the wonderful memories that go with it, so
he can save what Wall Street says he should save in order
to be rich thirty years from now?

Who knows, you could save all your life for that back-road
bicycle trip through France, only to find out those French
farmers went on strike again and are letting their cows
doodle on the road.

Enough talking about figuring out how much we
should save. Let's do it. The ten minutes you spend
completing the following work sheet will give you a
general idea of how much you need to save to successfully arrive at a financial goal sometime in the future,
assuming, of course, that you allocate these savings
effectively and at least approximate the return of the
stock market average with the assets you allocate to
common stocks.

It is impossible to know down to the last penny how your
investment decisions today will affect the size of your
portfolio when you are ready to retire. But completing
this work sheet will give you a general idea whether your
savings today are in the same universe as your retirement
expectations for tomorrow.

RETIREMENT WORK SHEET*

		35-yr-old with salary of $60,000	Your Numbers
1	ANNUAL INCOME NEEDED AT RETIREMENT IN TODAY'S DOLLARS (MULTIPLY CURRENT SALARY BY 90%)	$54,000	
2	SOCIAL SECURITY BENEFITS (CALL 800-722-1313 FOR ESTIMATE, OR USE 20% OF CURRENT SALARY)	$12,000	
3	RETIREMENT INCOME NEEDED (LINE 1 MINUS LINE 2)	$42,000	
4	AMOUNT OF MONEY NEEDED BY RETIREMENT IN TODAY'S DOLLARS (LINE 3 TIMES 20)	$840,000	
5	AMOUNT ALREADY SAVED FOR RETIREMENT	$120,000	
6	VALUE OF SAVINGS AT RETIREMENT IN TODAY'S DOLLARS (LINE 5 TIMES INVESTMENT GROWTH FACTOR; SEE FOLLOWING CHART)	$388,800	
7	SAVINGS STILL NEEDED IN TODAY'S DOLLARS (LINE 4 MINUS LINE 6)	$451,200	
8	MONTHLY AMOUNT YOU NEED TO SAVE (LINE 7 TIMES MONTHLY SAVINGS FACTOR LISTED ON CHART)	$677	

*Assumes retirement age at 65.

RETIREMENT WORK SHEET FACTORS

Your Age	Investment Growth Factor	Monthly Savings Factor
21	5.62	0.0007
23	5.19	0.0008
25	4.80	0.0009
27	4.44	0.0010
29	4.10	0.0011
31	3.79	0.0012
33	3.51	0.0013
35	3.24	0.0015
37	3.00	0.0017
39	2.77	0.0019
41	2.56	0.0021
43	2.37	0.0024
45	2.19	0.0028
47	2.03	0.0032
49	1.87	0.0038
51	1.73	0.0046
53	1.60	0.0055
55	1.48	0.0069
57	1.37	0.0090
59	1.27	0.0126
61	1.17	0.0196
63	1.08	0.0408

The best way to subtly remind yourself of the need to save is to make a copy of the work sheet and tape it somewhere, like your closet door, so that you see it day after day after day. If you have something reminding you day after day after day to do something about a potential financial crisis, eventually you will do something.

Fortunately for many people, this pending retirement problem is ten, twenty, or thirty years away. But even though this problem may be ten, twenty, or thirty years away, taking personal responsibility for our destiny means having the discipline to do something about it today, even if what you do today is nothing more than completing your work sheet and taping it to your closet door, because the longer you wait to tape it to the closet door the more you delay putting that work sheet into action.

The first step in being a responsible investor is to calculate an approximate savings goal. The next step is to implement your goal, if only a little at first. Following is a graph that points out the importance of saving earlier rather than later. It compares two individuals who save $300 monthly until they reach sixty-five years of age. One starts saving at age twenty-five and the other starts saving at age thirty-five.

The investor who starts saving and investing $300 monthly at age twenty-five instead of age thirty-five invests only $36,000 more but ends up with an additional $604,195 in her portfolio! If you are the thirty-five-year-old and want to start saving, remember that there is one thing much worse than starting to save at thirty-five instead of at twenty-five—and that is to not start at all. You can either sit there and wish you had done something ten years ago, or you can start doing something today and ten years from now look back and be glad you did!

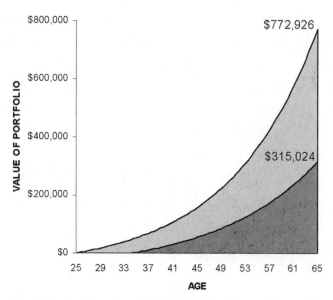

Example based on 7 percent growth in tax-deferred account.

This predicament of inaction is a funny thing, and I suspect many of us have been challenged by it in other areas of our lives in addition to saving and investing:

the inaction of wanting to apply for a new job but not updating the resume,

the inaction of wanting to learn a new skill but not signing up for a class,

the inaction of wanting to say "I'm sorry" to a friend you've hurt but not picking up the phone.

I have dealt with all of the above at one time or another in my life, and I suspect you have also, and isn't it funny that the longer you wait, the harder it is. BUT when inaction finally turns to action, we feel good about the action, whether or not the outcome is in line with our initial expectations, and we find ourselves saying,

"I'm glad I tried."

"I learned a lot."

"It wasn't as hard as I thought it would be."

"At least I know where I stand."

I'm convinced that those of you who take action in the form of saving enough will one day look back with the enormous feeling of accomplishment that usually results from doing something successfully that we know needs to be done.

The following table shows that when you increase your savings amount a little each month it makes a significant impact on the future value of your portfolio. It is a lot easier to save and invest a little more each month than to try to do it all at once at the end of the year.

While we're talking about the importance of saving, the most efficient way to do it is in a tax-deferred retirement

Monthly Investment	10 Years	20 Years	30 Years
$ 100	$ 15,814	$ 48,435	$ 113,343
$ 300	$ 47,443	$145,305	$ 340,029
$ 500	$ 79,072	$242,175	$ 566,716
$1,000	$158,143	$484,349	$1,133,431

Assumes 7 percent growth in tax-deferred account.

account, such as a company-sponsored retirement plan or your own IRA. When you start your savings program in a tax-deferred account, you are taking advantage of the enormous tax break Uncle Sam offers you by letting your savings grow tax deferred. And when you invest in a company-sponsored 401(k) plan, many companies will match a portion of your contribution, thus accentuating this tax-deferred growth.

I don't pretend to have all the right answers when it comes to saving enough for one's retirement, because the way we save and increase our savings is different for everyone. For some, sharing a dinner out with their spouse at the end of the month might be a reward for meeting their monthly budget. For others, having dinner out with their spouse might be the punishment for not meeting a monthly budget.

You never know.

The point of this chapter is not to give you a boatload of great savings ideas that you can incorporate into your daily life, like refinancing your home or reusing plastic sandwich bags four times before they are discarded.

Quite frankly, I use them only once.

But I never buy brand-new golf balls.

The point of this chapter is to create an awareness of how our saving today will impact us in the future. I am confident that when this awareness is firmly in place, our sense of personal responsibility, combined with our individual creativity and bright ideas, will find a way to get the job done.

7 LIFE, LOGIC, AND PARADOXES

LET'S TALK A LITTLE BIT ABOUT LIFE, LOGIC, LEARNING, investing, and paradoxes.

"Paradox" is one of those words we are 95 percent sure we know the meaning of but check the dictionary anyway. I'll save you the trouble.

par·a·dox (păr'-ə-dŏks') n. **1.** a seemingly contradictory statement that may nonetheless be true.[1]

Before we talk about the greatest investment paradox of all time, let's talk a little about life, logic, and learning.

In our journey through life, I think we can logically say that the more we learn, the better off we are. This observation fits neatly into the way we conduct our affairs, live our lives, and survive in this world. Whether it is learning a new subject in first grade, revamping a production line problem, or becoming a better parent, the more we learn, the better off we are.

However, when it comes to investing, you can kiss this logic good-bye, because the less time you spend trying to learn everything there is to know about stocks, bonds, and mutual funds, the better off you are. But you do need to know a few things, including how expenses and taxes affect your portfolio, and the lesson to learn is: The less you pay in expenses and taxes, the better off you are.

There you go. Class dismissed.

The second-greatest investment paradox of all time is that so many seemingly sophisticated mutual fund managers stick you with expenses and taxes year after year in the process of consistently underperforming the stock market average.

The greatest investment paradox of all time is that so many seemingly sophisticated investors continue to give these mutual fund managers bundles of money to do it again next year. By the time most investors realize what's going on, it's too late.

When you pay a mutual fund manager a few cents here and a few cents there in the form of annual operating expenses, and you pay the U.S. government a few cents here and a few cents there in the form of capital gains taxes resulting from all the trades done by your mutual fund manager, eventually a few cents here and a few cents there add up to thousands and thousands and hundreds of thousands of dollars, even in smaller accounts.

Good money.

Gone from your account forever.

It seems to me that we are so darned busy attending our children's activities, trying to squeeze in a vacation, and working on Saturdays that we rarely (if ever) take time to figure out how expenses and taxes impact our investments over time. Eventually, instead of having thousands and thousands of additional dollars at retirement to do the things we have always wanted to do, like put a down payment on a lake cabin, take an oil painting class, buy a motorcycle, travel with children and grandchildren, start a new business, or pay bills, we have paid thousands and thousands and hundreds of thousands of dollars to a mutual fund manager and the U.S. government in expenses and taxes.

That's not good.

I am not saying that an investor's main goal should be to avoid all expenses and taxes. I am simply showing you how excessive expenses and taxes impact a portfolio. You can take it from there.

Before reviewing the impact of a managed mutual fund's annual expenses, let me clarify one thing: Every mutual fund—including any unmanaged stock index fund—has annual expenses. I bring this to your attention only because, on more than one occasion, I have asked mutual fund investors what their funds' annual expenses are and they have replied, "I own a no-load. I don't have annual expenses."

They are wrong.

"No load" means no one-time commission on your mutual fund. "No load" does not mean you don't pay an annual mutual fund expense, because you do. If you don't believe me, look it up in your mutual fund's prospectus.

It doesn't matter what kind of mutual fund you own—no-loads, front-loads, back-loads, side-loads, top-loads, or bottom-loads—every mutual fund charges an annual expense. They don't send you a bill every month like your utility company does, but believe me, you pay it. Mutual fund companies simply collect their fee by reducing your price per share.

Maybe if mutual fund companies sent a bill each month, more investors would take the time to see whether they were getting their money's worth.

The easiest way to find out your mutual fund's annual expense is to call the company and ask. Or, better yet, look in your mutual fund's prospectus for a fee table, sometimes called an expenses table.

It will look something like this:

ANNUAL FUND OPERATING EXPENSES	
(as a percentage of average net assets)	
MANAGEMENT FEE	1.00%
12b-1 FEES	0.25%
OTHER EXPENSES	0.25%
TOTAL FUND EXPENSE	1.50%

The average expense ratio for a managed stock mutual fund is 1.41 percent of your money.[2] You can build an indexed portfolio for 0.25 percent of your money. Without overstating the obvious, that's about 80 percent less (not to mention that with an indexed mutual fund, you are also assured of at least approximating the stock market average).

I wonder whether one of the reasons so few investors pay attention to annual mutual fund expenses is that annual mutual fund expenses are quoted in warm and fuzzy numbers like 1 percent and 2 percent instead of enormously large numbers like $221,628.

Let's look at how annual mutual fund expenses affect you, not in warm and fuzzy numbers of 1 percent and 2 percent, but in numbers that most of us relate to—cold cash—because it's the cold cash of enormously large numbers, not warm and fuzzy percentages, that will be missing from our portfolios when we need it most.

Below is a table that shows the cold-cash impact that annual expenses have on a managed mutual fund compared

End of year	Value of stock index mutual fund with fees of 0.25%	Value of managed mutual fund with fees of 1.5%	Difference
1	$ 6,146	$ 6,128	$ 19
2	$ 12,906	$ 12,787	$ 119
3	$ 20,342	$ 20,024	$ 317
4	$ 28,520	$ 27,890	$ 629
5	$ 37,514	$ 36,439	$ 1,076
6	$ 47,407	$ 45,729	$ 1,678
7	$ 58,288	$ 55,826	$ 2,462
8	$ 70,256	$ 66,800	$ 3,456
9	$ 83,420	$ 78,726	$ 4,693
10	$ 97,897	$ 91,688	$ 6,210
11	$113,821	$105,774	$ 8,047
12	$131,336	$121,083	$10,252
13	$150,599	$137,722	$12,878
14	$171,787	$155,804	$15,983
15	$195,091	$175,457	$19,634

$500 monthly investment, assuming 10% annual return.

to an unmanaged stock index fund over a fifteen-year period.

You don't need to spend all day Saturday and half of Sunday poring over glossy mutual fund magazines to figure out which fund—a managed fund or an unmanaged index fund—has a leg up or down when it comes to annual mutual fund expenses.

It gets worse.

For younger investors who know that they might have an investment time horizon a little longer than fifteen years, the table on the next page shows the impact that annual mutual fund expenses have over a thirty-year period.

At first glance, annual operating expenses hidden deep in the middle of every mutual fund prospectus might seem like mere pocket change.

To anyone who thinks $221,628 is mere pocket change, I'd like to have your pockets.

Investing in a managed mutual fund is no laughing matter, unless you are a mutual fund manager; then you get to laugh all the way to the bank.

End of year	Value of stock index mutual fund with fees of 0.25%	Value of managed mutual fund with fees of 1.5%	Difference
16	$ 220,722	$196,815	$ 23,907
17	$ 248,913	$220,027	$ 28,886
18	$ 279,920	$245,254	$ 34,666
19	$ 314,024	$272,671	$ 41,352
20	$ 351,533	$302,468	$ 49,065
21	$ 392,790	$334,852	$ 57,937
22	$ 438,166	$370,047	$ 68,119
23	$ 488,075	$408,297	$ 79,778
24	$ 542,969	$449,867	$ 93,102
25	$ 603,345	$495,046	$108,299
26	$ 669,751	$544,146	$125,605
27	$ 742,790	$597,509	$145,280
28	$ 823,123	$655,504	$167,619
29	$ 911,480	$718,534	$192,947
30	$ 1,008,662	$787,034	$221,628

$500 monthly investment, assuming 10% annual return.

It is not unheard of for mutual fund managers to earn a million dollars or more each year while consistently underperforming the stock market average. The sad part is, the money you pay them to underperform the stock market average comes out of your retirement money. It's just that most investors are too busy to stop and calculate that $221,628 of their retirement money might be a little too much to pay someone to consistently underperform the stock market average.

Now for the scary part. In addition to annual mutual fund expenses, many investors also pay a financial adviser or stockbroker an annual management fee of 1.5 percent to 2 percent to select and then watch over their managed mutual funds.

I am not an expert in advanced trigonometry, but I am smart enough to figure out that when annual mutual fund expenses of 1 percent to 2 percent are combined with yearly advisory fees of 1 percent to 2 percent, many investors end up paying 2 percent to 3 percent of the total value of their portfolio in yearly expenses and fees.

When the stock market is returning 26 percent a year, it's easy to swallow 2 percent to 3 percent in expenses and fees. But when the stock market returns 10 percent to 11 percent a year (its historical average), 2 percent to 3 percent in expenses and fees eats up one fourth of your investment earnings.

I am not one to pass judgment, because if the financial industry can charge its customers 2 percent to 3 percent and get away with it, then let the good times roll. But if you want my humble opinion on the matter, giving up one fourth of our investment earnings each year in expenses and fees for something most of us can do better ourselves flat-out doesn't make sense. Below is a table that summarizes the impact of 2.5 percent in combined mutual fund expenses and advisory management fees over a thirty-year period.

End of year	Value of stock index mutual fund with fees of 0.25%	Value of managed account with fees of 3%	Difference
1	$ 6,146	$ 6,105	$ 41
2	$ 12,906	$ 12,645	$ 262
3	$ 20,342	$ 19,650	$ 691
4	$ 28,520	$ 27,155	$ 1,365
5	$ 37,514	$ 35,194	$ 2,320
6	$ 47,407	$ 43,806	$ 3,601
7	$ 58,288	$ 53,031	$ 5,257
8	$ 70,256	$ 62,913	$ 7,343
9	$ 83,420	$ 73,499	$ 9,920
10	$ 97,897	$ 84,839	$ 13,058
11	$ 113,821	$ 96,987	$ 16,835
12	$ 131,336	$110,000	$ 21,336
13	$ 150,599	$123,939	$ 26,660
14	$ 171,787	$138,872	$ 32,915
15	$ 195,091	$154,868	$ 40,223
16	$ 220,722	$172,004	$ 48,718
17	$ 248,913	$190,359	$ 58,554
18	$ 279,920	$210,023	$ 69,897
19	$ 314,024	$231,087	$ 82,937
20	$ 351,533	$253,651	$ 97,883
21	$ 392,790	$277,822	$114,967
22	$ 438,166	$303,715	$134,451
23	$ 488,075	$331,452	$156,623
24	$ 542,969	$361,165	$181,804
25	$ 603,345	$392,994	$210,351
26	$ 669,751	$427,090	$242,661
27	$ 742,790	$463,614	$279,175
28	$ 823,123	$502,740	$320,383
29	$ 911,480	$544,653	$366,827
30	$1,008,662	$589,551	$419,111

$500 monthly investment, assuming 10% annual return.

When making investment decisions today that will impact your long-term financial goals of tomorrow, it's tempting to focus on the latest, hottest, handsomest mutual fund manager profiled in your Sunday newspaper's business section. Maybe, instead, we should begin to focus on the $419,111 in cold cash that will be missing from our portfolios when we retire.

And don't forget, these hypothetical examples assume your financial adviser was able to choose for you a managed mutual fund portfolio that approximated the stock market average prior to subtracting expenses and fees.

That, my friend, is an awfully big assumption.

Which brings me to my next point, and for investors who have a desire to work with a financial adviser, you need to pay close attention. In chapters 3 and 4 we discovered how to successfully build and maintain a diversified common-stock portfolio on our own. However, many investors underestimate the complexities of creating a long-term financial plan, establishing an asset allocation that works for them, and then sticking with the plan in all types of markets. If you are the type who prefers the long-term guidance of a financial adviser when it comes to investing, *then do the right thing for yourself and hire a financial adviser to assist you.*

But never lose sight of what you are hiring her to do.

You should hire a financial adviser to help you develop and sustain your long-term financial plan. And remember, at the foundation of your plan are the three fundamental principles of investing—asset allocation, approximating the return of the stock market average, and an awareness of your saving and spending goals. You should not be hiring a financial adviser in order to try to beat the stock market average, unless of course that is your specific objective.

The yearly management fees you pay your financial adviser can be *worth every penny* if your financial adviser protects you from pushing all the wrong buttons and doing all the wrong things when the stock market moves a thousand points in either direction tomorrow. A financial adviser's fee is earned by making sure you adhere to your asset allocation and saving goals, not by using your money to attempt to beat the stock market average.

Fees and expenses are not the only thing eating into your portfolio's value. Taxes also have a significant impact on the value of your portfolio at retirement, and the strategy here is really quite simple: If you have an opportunity to reduce your taxes, do it.

How profound.

The most obvious way to reduce your tax bill is to invest in a tax-deferred account, such as an IRA or 401(k) plan, and have your investments grow tax deferred.

The second way to reduce your tax bill is to own indexed mutual funds instead of managed mutual funds when investing in regular (taxable) accounts. How does this reduce your tax bill? Let me explain.

As a mutual fund owner, you are taxed on any profits made when you sell your shares. You are also taxed on the net profits your mutual fund manager generates from all his buying and selling activities—regardless of whether you receive these gains in cash or reinvest them in additional shares.

It goes without saying that if your mutual fund manager is caught up in BUYING LOTS OF THIS and SELLING LOTS OF THAT throughout the year, all his BUY THIS and SELL THAT activity will generate a capital gains tax liability much higher than the capital gains tax generated from an unmanaged index fund. That's because an index fund simply lets the shares in the fund sit there and do nothing much but grow and compound.

Let's take a closer look.

A mutual fund's "turnover ratio" is a statistic that gives you a general idea of all the buying and selling activity that goes on within the fund. A mutual fund that has a 50 percent turnover ratio (over the course of a year) can generally be expected to replace (turn over) 50 percent of the portfolio's value.

A mutual fund that has a 100 percent turnover ratio can be expected to replace 100 percent of its value over the course of a year. The table below[3] lists the turnover ratios of three categories of managed fund groups and compares them to the turnover ratio of index funds.

FUND CATEGORY	TURNOVER RATIO
LARGE-CAP FUNDS	68%
VANGUARD S&P 500 INDEX FUND	5%
MID-CAP FUNDS	102%
VANGUARD MID-CAP INDEX FUND	19%
SMALL-CAP FUNDS	98%
VANGUARD SMALL-CAP FUNDS	16%

Even though there isn't a direct correlation between the turnover ratio and capital gains tax liability, the turnover ratio gives you a general idea of the buy/sell activity within a mutual fund—activity that is certain to impact your total return after Uncle Sam gets his chunk of the action. In addition, the buy/sell activity of the fund increases the internal commissions paid out, on top of the performance drag the fund absorbs resulting from the bid/ask spread inherent in buying and selling stocks.

Obviously, when it comes to investing in a regular (taxable) account, it pays to consider owning unmanaged stock index funds, which generally have much lower turnover ratios—and therefore tend to generate smaller capital gains taxes and less internal fees—than managed mutual funds.

Life, logic, learning, investing, and paradoxes.

Oh, and don't forget hoopla.

hoop·la (hōōp'-lä') n. Slang. **l.** Boisterous commotion or excitement. 2. Talk intended to mislead or confuse.[4]

With all the hoopla surrounding what the economy did yesterday, what the stock market did today, and which funds to own tomorrow as a result of what happened yesterday and today, don't forget about the expenses and taxes in your portfolio.

If you take the time to figure out how much it costs you, not in warm and fuzzy percentages, but in real dollars, I think you will find that minimizing your expenses and taxes is worth the effort it takes to do it.

8 TRAVELS OF A COFFEEHOUSE INVESTOR

I HATE TO LOSE MONEY, BUT IT DIDN'T MATTER TO ME when I was a kid, because I didn't have much money to lose. I wanted to get rich.

I am not quite sure how that yearning to get rich got hold of me at such a young age. Maybe it was a result of growing up in a prosperous farming community in eastern Washington State that sometimes got a little too caught up in the latest large combines, fast boats, big trucks, and yes, hot stocks.

The farm we grew up on wasn't just any farm. It was the best dry-land farm in the world, nestled on the breaks of the Snake River Canyon in a corner of the world *National Geographic* once eloquently described as a "Paradise called the Palouse." And despite all the heartaches that were a part of farming back then, the farmers in that corner of paradise took great pride in consistently producing more wheat than any other county in the nation, thanks to those soft springtime rains in May.

Anyway, after my third year in college it began to dawn on me that I wasn't going to get rich by returning to the farm after graduation and working as my dad's hired hand at four dollars an hour, especially when I had three younger brothers competing with me for that same seat on the combine. That was the summer I packed my bags, threw them in the back of my Chevy Nova, and took off for the big city of Chicago. I figured if I couldn't get rich sitting on a combine harvesting wheat in paradise, maybe I could make my fortune trading wheat futures in the pits of the Chicago Board of Trade. It was a start, anyway, and quite an adventurous one at that, allowing a farm boy from the Palouse a chance to ride the elevated subways of Chicago and grow up pretty fast.

The truth was, I had discovered my own paradise. Instead of chopping thistles on hot August afternoons back on the farm, I was catching afternoon Cubs games on the north side of Chicago on my way home from work.

During the day, I was a floor clerk at the Board of Trade, but evenings were a different story. I spent my time in Northwestern University's computer lab writing technical trading systems to simulate my fortunes trading wheat. After four months of fine-tuning a twenty-day moving average program, I opened a commodities account to trade in real time, and you can guess the rest of the story; I lost my entire life's savings in one week of trading wheat futures.

The bad news is that all the money I had saved up from working on the farm was gone. The good news is that I discovered that I hated to lose money a lot more than I wanted to get rich, and never again did I try to outsmart the wheat market, or the stock market, or any other type of market.

That humbling incident stuck with me as I graduated from college and started my career as a stockbroker in Seattle. Instead of opening up a trading account for myself to buy and sell stocks, I started socking away money in my company's 401(k) plan in a large-cap mutual fund. Ten years later, without my so much as picking one stock, and with my barely having looked at my account all those years, my retirement account had grown to a nice little sum of money.

Although I let go of that urge to get rich early on in my life, I still had a desire to build financial wealth and buy some nice things, first for myself, and later for my family. And I have to admit, growing up and living in a country that openly promotes an abundance of consumption, over the years I have had to stop and ask myself, "When is enough

enough?" amid the competing tugs of spending it today or saving it for a financially secure future.

When is enough enough? In dealing with this sensitive topic of finding a balance in a country that promotes an abundance of consumption, I am drawn to the first verse of "The Spell of the Yukon" in a poetry book by Robert Service that I take with me when climbing the mountains of the Pacific Northwest.

> *I wanted the gold, and I sought it;*
> *I scrabbled and mucked like a slave.*
> *Was it famine or scurvy, I fought it;*
> *I hurled my youth into a grave.*
> *I wanted the gold, and I got it—*
> *Came out with a fortune last fall,—*
> *Yet somehow life's not what I thought it,*
> *and somehow the gold isn't all.*

When is enough enough? Most of us have probably dealt with that question at one time or another in our lives, pursuing that pot of gold, and enjoying the journey along the way, but there comes a time when we finally do realize that the energy spent with families and friends and communities is more fulfilling than an endless pursuit of that pot of gold.

The reason I am discussing this is that even though you might have answered the question of "When is enough

enough?" in your personal life, I have worked with enough investors to recognize that it can be a whole lot harder to answer that question when making investment decisions in your personal portfolio.

Putting your pursuit of higher returns in perspective with your investments, especially with the money you have invested in common stocks, so that you have a clear understanding of when enough is enough, is essential for your long-term financial well-being. With thousands of actively managed mutual funds and thousand of stocks available to choose from, you are certain to always come across a few stocks and mutual funds that have been generating returns far better than the ones you currently own.

Should you stay put or should you switch?

When is enough enough? I don't pose this question lightly. In the coming years investors are likely to struggle with this question like never before. Here's why.

For seventeen years, from 1983 through 1999, the Standard and Poor's 500 stock index generated an annualized return of just over 18 percent, about 80 percent above its long-term average. In this era of oversized returns, the question "When is enough enough?" might not have seemed all that important. You could buy and sell lots of stocks and mutual funds in pursuit of performance during those years and still come out ahead, even if it meant you ended up like most investors with an annualized return of only 12 percent—six percentage points less than what the market offered you.[1]

Keep in mind though, that if the stock market can generate a seventeen-year period of oversized returns it can also generate a seventeen-year period of underperforming the market. While we are on the topic of having to endure a seventeen-year period of underperformance, it might be interesting to note that we are halfway through it. For the past eight and one half years, the stock market has generated a return of nothing.

This is where Wall Street enters the picture.

When the stock market happens to be going through a prolonged period of subdued returns, the financial industry, knowing that many investors haven't answered the question "When is enough enough?," cozies up to you and whispers in your ear . . .

"You can do better than that."

On top of that, Wall Street, ever mindful of the threat index funds pose to its livelihood of selling top stocks and mutual funds, is especially aggressive at applying these sales tactics to investors who embrace the simple concept of indexing in their common-stock portfolio. You have heard the pitch before, and it goes something like this . . .

Index funds work great in bull markets, but not in bear markets.
Our professional stock pickers will protect you in a down market.
Why settle for "average" when you can invest in our fantastic five-month track record?

In your desire to own a successful common stock portfolio, Wall Street implies that it wants to help you achieve your goals. But never forget that Wall Street's financial goals frequently collide with your financial goals, especially when you voice your intent to stay committed to your financial game plan that includes low-cost index funds and capture the market's long-term return.

That is *not* what they want to hear.

In coming to grips with Wall Street's short-term intentions and your long-term goals, let's explore some of the obstacles you will face if you succumb to Wall Street's whisper, "You can do better than that."

To invest in the stock market, you have one of three choices.

Individual stocks
Actively managed mutual funds
Index funds

Which choice is best for you? A good way to begin answering that question is to keep in mind the words of John F. Kennedy, who once said:

The great enemy of the truth is very often not the lie— deliberate, contrived, and dishonest, but the myth—persistent, persuasive, and unrealistic.

There are two myths of investing in the stock market that are persistent, persuasive, and unrealistic. The first myth is that great companies make great investments. The second myth is that a stockbroker, mutual fund manager, or any other stockpicking expert, like your father or co-worker, can consistently pick enough good stocks and avoid enough bad stocks to outperform the stock market average, which is made up of all the good and bad stocks combined.

Let's look at the first myth first.

When you purchase stock in a company, logically you would expect to benefit from the financial fortunes of that company through appreciation of the stock price and any dividends paid out. Because we like to think of ourselves as fairly logical in our decision making, it is extremely difficult, and in many cases impossible, for some investors to let go of that logic and accept the fact that all too often there is no connection between the financial fortunes of a company and its stock price. There are times when a great company's stock does great, but there are also times when a great company's stock does badly, and the same holds true for poorly run companies.

The reason why this occurs is that a company's stock price is not determined by the company itself; it is determined by the emotions of investors who buy and sell the company's stock.

Did you catch that? The reason there is no connection between the financial fortunes of a company and its stock price is that the stock's price is not determined by the company itself; it is determined by the emotions of investors who buy and sell the company's stock.

Okay, one more time . . . Oftentimes the stock price of a company moves randomly in relation to the financial fortunes of a company because the stock's price is not determined by the company itself; it is determined by the emotions of investors who buy and sell the company's stock.

For instance, when a company announces quarterly earnings that are five times greater than last year's earnings, frequently the good news causes the price of its stock to drop. Why? Because, with thousands of investors weighing in through their buy and sell decisions, the impressive quarterly earnings report has already been built in to the price of the stock. In other words, the stock market is fairly efficient at pricing in current and future information before it takes place.

(Notice I said "fairly" efficient, not "totally" efficient, but more on that later.)

What about companies and stock prices over a longer period of time? Are the same types of short-run efficiencies on display in the long run? To answer that question, let's look at a company that is headquartered in a neighborhood next to mine.

Microsoft went public in May 1987, and for the next fourteen years the company's stock price grew a lot faster than the underlying earnings of the company. Maybe that was because the investors' excitement got ahead of the company's earnings, which is often the case when a great company has lots of good stuff going on.

In 2000, this trend reversed itself. Since then, Microsoft's earnings have grown a lot faster than the investors' excitement. In fact, the company's stock price hasn't grown at all, it has declined. During this stretch, the company's earnings have increased by about 50 percent, while the company's stock price has declined by about 50 percent.

To put it bluntly, over the past eight years there has been a complete disconnect between the success of the company and its stock price.

Maybe the next time your stockbroker, your mutual fund manager, or you start looking at the earnings reports of a company, a better idea might be to start analyzing the emotions of the thousands of investors who want to buy or sell stock of that company, and then tabulate those emotions out over the next eight years to determine whether the company's stock is worth purchasing.

In the end, it doesn't matter if you purchase a good company or a bad company. What matters is the timing of when you buy the company and when you sell it, which brings me to the second myth of investing in the stock market.

Wall Street will forever promote the myth that through exhaustive research, stockbrokers and mutual fund managers can buy and sell enough good companies and bad companies over time to outperform the stock market average, which consists of both the good and bad companies combined. At the heart of this myth is the question of whether or not the stock market is efficient. It is a question, or debate, that will never go away. It is an interesting debate, I guess, if you don't have anything better to do with your time. If you stop to think about it, the debate is meaningless.

On one side of this great debate is Wall Street and its throng of stock pickers who claim to be experts in their profession. They work hard at trying to convince us that although it is a difficult job, it is possible to beat the stock market average. Worse than that, they try to persuade us that our long-term financial well-being is dependent on their stock-picking prowess.

On the other side of this great debate is a lineup of academicians, economists, a few distinguished investors, and a whole bunch of Coffeehouse Investors who, after poring over performance numbers, have concluded that anyone's success at beating the market is more attributable to random luck than stock-picking skill.

Put another way, in a forest full of one thousand coin-flipping chimps, a few of them are likely to flip heads ten times in a row. Skilled or lucky? I'll let you answer that on your own.

This great debate will never go away. It will never stop. In the end, whether the stock market is efficient or not is irrelevant to investors because it is the wrong question. The question to ask yourself is "What is the price I pay if I try to beat the market by exploiting any inefficiences . . .

and fail?"

For investors who do take on the challenge of finding market inefficiencies through individual stock selection or actively managed mutual funds in an attempt to beat the market, sooner or later your investments will under-perform the market average. It might happen next week, next month, next year, or ten years from now, and this underperformance will last a week, a month, a year, a de-cade, or more, but inevitably, its day will come. When it does, you will have to decide whether or not to stay put with your underperforming investments or switch to an-other top stock picker and another five-star track record.

Do you stay put or do you switch?

If you have struggled with this dilemma in the past, rest assured, you are not alone.

Board members of large endowment funds and state and corporate pension accounts grapple with this quandary as well: whether to fire an underperforming fund man-ager, as dictated in their investment policy statement, and hire someone else with a stellar track record.

Do you stay put or do you switch?

For fifteen consecutive years, Legg Mason's Value Trust Fund, managed by Wall Street's legendary stock picker

Bill Miller, beat the S&P 500 index. He was hailed as one of Wall Street's best, and anyone who argued *against* the efficiency of stock markets was quick to bring up Bill's name.

As I mentioned earlier, this outperformance couldn't last forever, and for investors in Legg Mason's Value Trust, it didn't. For the past thirty months the mutual fund has underperformed the S&P 500 index by over 30 percent, and who knows if the fund's (mis)fortunes are about to change anytime soon.[2]

I am not about to criticize Bill Miller for his stock-picking prowess. Maybe he is a good stock picker, and maybe he isn't. I certainly want to congratulate him on his track record from 1994 through 2005, because that is quite an accomplishment. This is only meant to expose the many challenges of managing a common-stock portfolio when you haven't decided when enough is enough.

Do you switch, or do you stay put?

If you stay put, you do so at your own peril and face the possibility that your stock picker might continue to underperform by another 30 percent over the next thirty months. If you switch, you are entering into the dangerous trap of pursuing past performance numbers, because the next star stock picker you select will inevitably underperform, be it a week, a month, or a decade later, and the buy-high-sell-low cycle continues. It didn't work in the wheat market and doesn't work in the stock market.

Will the stock market continue to underperform over the next nine years, as it has the past nine years? I am not predicting it, but I am emotionally preparing for it. Let's say the stock market *does* underperform, and generates annualized returns of 6 percent to 8 percent over the next decade. Is that not enough for you? If you succumb to Wall Street's whisper, "You can do better than that," there is a good chance your efforts at reaching for higher returns will cause you to end up with negative returns, or returns substantially lower than the stock market average, as was the case with many investors during the years 1983 to 1999.

What happens if I prepare for lower returns and I am wrong—the stock market begins another seventeen-year period of extraordinary returns? My common-stock portfolio of index funds is positioned to capture the same.

Although I didn't realize it then, looking back on my early years of losing money trading wheat futures and then making it back in my 401(k) account, those experiences had a profound impact on the way I look at risk and return and my overall approach to building wealth. It has never made much sense to me that so many investors are willing to take on all the risk inherent in common stocks, only to miserably underperform the stock market because they haven't answered the question, When is enough enough?

Speaking of failures, over the years I have experienced a lot of failures in my life, including businesses and marriages, but I can say that the failures I endured played an integral role in many of my successes, because life usually offers you an opportunity for a second chance when you fail, and a shot at doing things right the second time around.

Life can give you a second chance on a lot of things, but it does not turn back the clock. I was fortunate to learn about market efficiencies early on in life, even if it cost me my life's savings in the pits of the Chicago Board of Trade.

There will always be someone in your life, whether it be a stockbroker, a spouse, a father, or a coworker, who tells you that picking stocks and choosing actively managed funds in an attempt to beat the market is the best way to build long-term wealth. You can be sure that this rhetoric will increase in proportion to the length of subdued returns in the stock market. If you make the wrong decisions with your investments over the next ten years, life will give you a second chance to make the right choices you could have made today, but it won't give you back those ten years.

When it comes to investing, time is the most valuable asset class of all.

9 SPENDING IT

SOMETIMES I WONDER WHAT I COULD HAVE ACCOM-plished in life if I had the tenacity of my kid brother.

By the age of seventeen, he'd had enough of those hot August afternoons chopping thistles on the farm. It was time to become an airplane pilot. This brother of mine wanted to fly an airplane so badly that he bought himself a high school graduation present, an ultralight airplane kit—you know, those big, gliderlike contraptions with lawn mower–sounding engines that waddle through the sky.

After harvest was over, he and I cleared out our farm shop of combines and tractor parts, hauled in the ultralight airplane kit, laid out the plans on the bench, and went to work. It took us about seven days to build that airplane, and I remember that the last thing we did was make sure that the bolts that held the propeller to the engine were snug.

Then came the big day when we opened the shop door and pushed the airplane out onto the farmyard driveway. Although there wasn't any of the fanfare that greets Boeing's introduction of a new Dreamliner jetliner, the exhilaration and excitement of fifty thousand aerospace engineers were stuffed into the hearts of two farm boys.

(You might be wondering right about now where our parents were to be letting this adventure get so far, but they would probably just tell you that with eight kids running around on the farm, it wasn't the first time they lost track of two.)

It came time for my brother to put on an old football helmet and strap himself into the seat, and with a thumbs-up sign, I cranked the propeller and off he went.

The airplane, with my brother seated in the open cockpit, went zooming down the farmyard driveway before I had much of a chance to wish him good luck and then started lifting off the ground at about the same time I realized we had a big problem on our hands. . . .

My brother had never taken a flight training class

and I had never taken a first aid class.

Up until that point, I also had never given any thought to becoming an aerospace engineer, but even I could tell that the ultralight airplane was climbing too fast to maintain any type of sustained flight, and so, being the good big brother that I was, I started screaming at the top of my lungs, "Cut the power!"

He says he never heard me screaming because the engine was so loud and things were happening so fast, but eventually he did cut the power and started to descend at a glide path that even I could calculate wasn't conducive to a successful touchdown, and so I started screaming, "Pull up!" Eventually he did, and gently crash-landed on the hillside of a wheat field behind our farmyard shop.

As I was running up to the scene of the accident, he was climbing out of that cockpit, pulling off his helmet, and dusting himself off, and I could see he had a grin on his face that stretched from ear to ear. He might have crashed his ultralight, but hey, at least he got to pilot an airplane.

I think that crash knocked some sense into him, because the next thing he did was enroll in a flight training school, figuring that if he was going to become a commercial airline pilot, he had to start somewhere. A year later I was his first passenger as we climbed into a little two-seater and took off from the local airport with a direction of due south and a destination of Hell's Canyon in southern Idaho.

For one afternoon at least, we were living life large.

Every now and then when I board a commercial jetliner and peer into the cockpit, I reflect on those early years with my brother and get a little overwhelmed at the number of controls placed in front of the pilot and copilot compared to the throttle and joystick on that ultralight airplane.

Now, I might be going out on a limb here, but I have worked with enough investors in my lifetime as a financial adviser to know that if you are peering into this thing called retirement and get a little overwhelmed at the number of financial issues in front of you during this phase of your life, you are not alone.

Let's face it, if the experts can't agree on when you should take social security, whether you should have long-term care insurance, a realistic portfolio growth rate, a sensible withdrawal rate, and reasonable inflation figures . . . how confident are you of flying that big bird of yours through retirement?

Fortunately there is a tool that my brother uses to assist him in flying commercial jetliners, and this tool, or at least the concept behind it, is a tool you will want to master. It is the most important planning tool you will ever use to smooth out the financial turbulence you will encounter throughout your retirement years.

It is called an autopilot.

As my brother explains it, the autopilot is a tool that makes adjustments to the jetliner throughout the trip after the initial flight plan is filed prior to takeoff. During the flight there are many factors that will alter the airplane's route, like changes in wind speed, fuel burn rate, or bad weather at the arriving airport, requiring the autopilot to make changes along the way based on unforeseen factors so that the jetliner has a good-looking glide path toward touchdown at its final destination.

This simple concept of establishing a flight plan (but in your case it is called a financial plan) *and then making adjustments along the way* based on life changes and market fluctuations is an absolute must if you want to have any chance of maintaining a standard of living throughout your retirement years comparable to the one you are living today.[1]

Establish a financial plan and make adjustments along the way—it sounds simple enough, and most financial pundits promote it endlessly. But I have noticed that despite all the talk about financial plans, the thought of establishing one can be so overwhelming that most investors and stockbrokers end up discussing things that are a little easier to talk about, like what the Dow did today and what the Fed will do next week.

I guess that doesn't surprise me, because those are the things Wall Street loves to talk about, and even I have to admit these topics can be a little more interesting to discuss than how your financial burn rate (expenses) affects your glide path throughout retirement. On top of that, many of us have a tendency to avoid talking about issues that can be a little turbulent to hash out with a spouse, a loved one, or even ourselves.

As I mentioned in chapter 4, building a common-stock portfolio can be an immensely gratifying experience, especially when compared to building a space shuttle.

But I am not going to sugarcoat anything here.

There is a big difference between building a successful common-stock portfolio and successfully navigating a financial plan throughout your retirement years.

One is simple and straightforward. The other is complicated and turbulent.

One can be as simple as owning two or three low-cost index funds and rebalancing once a year.

The other requires that you combine things such as social security, pension income, taxes, unforeseen health care costs, inflation, supplemental Medicare insurance, potential elder care costs, distributions from tax-deferred accounts, part-time work, Roth IRAs, portfolio volatility, estate planning, life expectancy, asset allocation, and of course the most important subject of all, your monthly burn rate . . .

and then monitoring these inputs within a successful financial plan throughout your retirement years so your glide path to touchdown is the one you want it to be.

It is hard enough to figure out how to combine all those inputs into a financial plan before takeoff, but when you know that many of the inputs are going to be changing from month to month and year to year throughout your retirement years, a "what's the use?" feeling can creep into your efforts at establishing a flight plan. Before you know it, you are off doing something else more fun or more pressing; anything to avoid that turbulent feeling of establishing your own retirement plan.

However, creating that flight plan and then changing those inputs along the way is a whole lot more valuable than winging it through your retirement years with no plan at all. For instance, one of the planning inputs that will have a significant impact on your financial well-being twenty years out is the rate of inflation you put into your financial projection work sheet today, but what number should you use—3 percent, 4 percent, or 5 percent inflation? And with medical costs increasing at a rate twice the core rate of inflation, should you consider six?

What happens if you enter 6 percent and it turns out to be 3?

What happens if you enter 3 percent and it turns out to be 6?

In the above scenario, if you don't make any adjustments along the way, your financial glide path will either soar to the moon or crash and burn, but it won't touch down anywhere near what you projected. *But* if you have embraced the concept of autopilot, whether you enter 6 percent or 3 percent doesn't matter nearly as much as keeping track of your burn rate and then updating your burn rate amount each year in your flight plan to reflect the increase or decrease in your household expenses. You might find that it makes more sense to quit using the government's core inflation figure (which nobody can figure out anyway) in your plan and start inputting your personal inflation figure into your financial planning projections.

There are times in my life when I contemplate starting a project that seems almost too overwhelming to start, like writing a book, training for a marathon, or building a radio-controlled biplane with a six-foot wingspan and what seems like a thousand little wooden pieces, but I keep close at heart a suggestion by Mark Twain, who said that the secret to getting ahead is getting started, and so I begin.

And you must too, if the idea of having a successful financial plan throughout retirement appeals to you, even though reading this chapter overwhelms you right now.

To get ahead, you need to get started, and I have a suggestion on where to begin.

It works for me,
it works for investors I work with,
and I know it will work for you.

It is the easiest and most difficult component of your financial plan and it is the one aspect of your plan over which you have complete control.

Start by keeping track of your monthly burn rate.

When it comes to filing a flight plan, there are lots of inputs that will impact the outcome, but there is one that matters most of all, and that is how much you spend and what you spend it on during retirement.

That burn rate, which nobody wants to talk about, is what I want to talk about next. For some, keeping track of their expenses might have a "money management 101," constraining kind of feel to it, which I suspect has evolved over the years from getting caught up in this day-to-day thing called life.

On top of that, for much of the past quarter century, we have been accustomed to making money in our occupations, in the stock market, and maybe even in real estate markets. During those years of stellar returns, we were so consumed with making money and getting ahead and focusing on families and careers and communities that we ended up a little too busy during the day and a little too exhausted at day's end to keep track of how we spent the money we made.

And it wouldn't surprise me if this oversight that evolved during your working years has carried over to your retirement years.

Another reason there might be a reluctance to keep track of how we spend our money is that deep down, this action can have a restricting kind of feeling to it, corresponding closely to a budgeting mentality.

I hate budgets as much as you do, but keeping track of expenses has nothing to do with budgeting and everything to do with creating an awareness of how I spend my money. I have discovered that this awareness isn't restricting; it is incredibly freeing and powerful because it allows you to zero in on whether or not your expenses, *especially those that are discretionary,* are aligned with your desires and ambitions for your retirement years. Are you spending your financial resources in a way that reflects why you worked so hard to save them in the first place? Only you can answer that, and only after you have first identified what you are spending them on.

Throughout this discussion of burn rates and financial plans, we haven't talked much about price-earnings ratios and market cycles, because from an investing standpoint we have already discovered the most effective way to maximize your stock market returns over time is through low-cost index funds.

That isn't the only benefit of owning index funds.

From a financial planning standpoint, a far greater benefit of owning low-cost index funds is that it liberates you from having to dwell on economic numbers and quarterly earnings reports and other things Wall Street likes to talk about that are insignificant to your financial well-being. Instead, you can focus on things that are in your control, like your monthly burn rate, your retirement date, or part-time work throughout your retirement years.

And, contrary to popular opinion, I have found that the majority of investors enjoy that liberating feeling of ignoring Wall Street and focusing on things that actually matter to their flight plan. The feeling of being in control of one's financial destiny is infinitely more gratifying than having this sinking feeling that that big bird of yours is on a glide path to crash and burn.

When you start to keep track of your burn rate—how much you spend and what you spend it on—you take the essential first step to be in charge of your financial future throughout retirement. When you get right down to it, the big question on retirees' minds is also the one factor that affects the glide path most of all: "How much money can I withdraw from my portfolio today without running out of money in twenty or thirty years?" A difficult question, to be sure, compounded by the fact that most retirees, even those with a million dollars or more in their investment accounts, won't be able to support their current lifestyle on just the income and growth of their investment portfolio. They will be forced to nibble away at the principal over time if they want to maintain their current lifestyle throughout their retirement years. And there is nothing wrong with nibbling away at the principal of your portfolio, as long as you don't nibble too fast.

How fast is too fast?

Once that key component (your burn rate) is entered in your flight plan, it allows you to make a projection regarding how long your money will last based on how much you draw out of your portfolio each month to supplement other types of income, like social security or pensions.

But that is just the beginning. Another component to your flight plan that will impact how much money you can withdraw from your portfolio each month and how long your money will last is the rate of growth of your portfolio, and that figure will depend largely on how you allocate your investment portfolio between stocks, bonds, money market funds, real estate, and other asset classes in your overall portfolio mix.

Here is where your flight plan proves invaluable, because now you can make some portfolio decisions, like how to allocate your assets between stocks and bonds, based not on some arbitrary percentage, but on your ability and need to take on additional risk in your portfolio in pursuit of higher returns to reach your goals.

For instance, should you invest most of your money in safe and secure things like CDs or highly rated bonds to protect against a substantial decline in the stock market, or do you put most of your money in safe and secure things like the stock market to protect against inflation and substantial loss of purchasing power twenty years from now?

How about investing in a little of both?

Your financial plan provides an awareness of your choices, like whether you are better off reducing your monthly burn rate to live with the lower returns attached to a more conservative portfolio, or whether you are emotionally willing and financially able to absorb a steep stock market decline in pursuit of higher returns.

What is the right asset allocation for you? There are so many factors that go into answering that question and so much information available on the subject and so many Monte Carlo models claiming to have the best allocation formula for the perfect allocation that I would need to possess more than the tenacity of my kid brother to waddle into that discussion in this chapter. In the end, there is no right or wrong allocation, but your financial plan will do a good job of determining an approximate allocation that works for you based on your need for higher returns and emotional ability to endure short-term losses in your portfolio.

I will offer an observation that has come from connecting with countless Coffeehouse Investors who are retired and, like you, are faced with the dual challenge of enduring today's stock market volatility while addressing the inevitability of increased burn rates and inflationary pressures over the next decade and beyond.

Once you have settled on an approximate allocation that works for you, whether it is a 45 percent, 50 percent, or

55 percent allocation to stocks or bonds, fine-tuning this allocation every three months isn't nearly as important as keeping track of your monthly burn rate and financial plan so your big bird glides through retirement at a rate that is right for you.

10 INDEX FUNDS AND BEYOND

ITS TIME HAD COME.

The evolution of index funds as a simple and sophisticated way to invest in the stock market can be traced back beyond 1971, but that happened to be the year that a major bank created the first index fund for the employee pension account of the Samsonite company.

It wasn't too long after that, in 1976 to be exact, when John Bogle, founder and retired chairman of Vanguard, offered the first retail index fund to investors like you and me. His actions provoked harsh ridicule from the financial community for his promotion of a simple concept that allowed investors to match the market's return and ignore Wall Street.

This criticism comes as no surprise to me, because during my days as a stockbroker with a Wall Street brokerage firm, at times it seemed like our total existence was measured on the volume of commissions we generated by selling top-performing stocks and mutual funds to our clients. Come to think of it, I am not sure anyone in my office even knew that an S&P 500 index fund existed. The stockbrokers in my office were too caught up in promoting the best companies recommended by the firm's top stock analysts.

When I look back on those years, I have to admit I was never very good at selling stocks to my investor clients. Maybe it was because I soon figured out there wasn't any correlation between our analysts' top stock picks and how those stocks performed. But it didn't matter anyway, because most of my clients were more interested in buying tax-free municipal bonds. Back in the 1980s, I found it a lot easier to sell triple-A-rated, tax-free bonds yielding 7 percent than to try to peddle the stock of some new company whose main product was a stuffed teddy bear named Teddy Ruxpin.

One day my largest municipal bond client threw me for a loop when he called me up and instructed me to wire a large chunk of his money to a company called Vanguard to be invested in its S&P 500 index fund, and so I did.

I didn't ponder his request much after that, I just kept on selling tax-free municipal bonds to clients from coast to coast. A few years later, though, I decided that it was time to move on from this business of being a stockbroker and bond salesman and do something else with my life. Thirteen years was enough for me. I was bored stiff and thinking to myself that I didn't really want to spend the rest of my life selling municipal bonds.

So I walked away from the brokerage firm, which meant I needed to roll my 401(k) account into a self-directed IRA. A spirited discussion about market efficiencies with my brother-in-law, who had just completed his MBA at the University of Washington, combined with my client's investment in Vanguard's S&P 500 index fund persuaded me to take a leap of faith and send my money to Vanguard.

I was an unemployed ex-stockbroker with lots of time on my hands exploring what to do next with my life. The more time I spent reflecting on what went on at that brokerage firm and trying to rationalize it against my IRA investment in Vanguard's S&P 500 index fund, the more I realized that an enormous opportunity existed to highlight the logic of index funds, which John Bogle had championed almost twenty years earlier.

I had a sense that for every investor who was caught up in finding the next hot stock or mutual fund, there were probably thousands, if not millions, of investors, like my seven brothers and sisters, who would see beyond the hype of Wall Street if presented with a logical alternative.

That is how the Coffeehouse Investor came about.

It was an idea whose time had come. And thanks to the thousands, if not millions, of investors who now embrace the logic of owning index funds, the idea continues to unfold.

The simple concept of index funds continues to spread out across the investment landscape embraced enthusiastically by individual investors, begrudgingly by Wall Street.

Investors are realizing what I did: that the secret to building a successful common-stock portfolio isn't to "beat the stock market" over the next two years, it is to capture its entire return over the next two decades.

Wall Street firms, realizing that thousands, if not millions, of investors are turning away from top stocks and managed funds to embrace index funds, have concluded that in order to keep from losing fees and commissions, they had better act fast and come up with something remotely connected to index funds. Wall Street is intent on making a buck or two on anything, even if it means making a buck by turning a good idea into a bad idea, and that is what they are doing with index funds.

In a nutshell, Wall Street has taken the index fund, and, piggybacking on all the goodwill that has been built up in these investments by the efforts of John Bogle and others, has turned the idea inside out and upside down by creating one thousand and more "sector" index funds that you can buy and sell to beat the stock market average.

In the good old days, Wall Street would try to sell you on the importance of owning the top stocks and mutual funds as crucial to your financial success. Now the financial industry has cranked up its marketing machine once again to sell you on the importance of investing in the top industries through "sector index funds" as crucial to your financial success.

In your desire to build wealth, ignore Wall Street, and get on with your life, it is time to revisit the coffeehouse to learn more about the difference between some of the good things and some of the bad things that are taking place in the evolution of index funds.

Without question, the most revolutionary product surrounding index funds has been the introduction of exchange-traded index funds, commonly referred to as ETFs. Exchange-traded funds are similar to traditional index mutual funds with one major difference; ETFs are shares of interest in index mutual funds and are bought and sold throughout the day on stock exchanges like the New York Stock Exchange and the American Stock Exchange. Traditional (index) mutual funds are purchased or redeemed once a day, either directly with the mutual fund provider, like Fidelity or Vanguard, or through a third-party mutual fund supermarket like Charles Schwab, and receive only the closing price at the end of that day's trading.

The first exchange-traded fund, the Standard & Poor's Depository Receipt, commonly known as a SPDR, or "spider," started trading in 1993 and mirrors the performance of S&P 500 index. It can be argued that the construction of ETFs is superior to traditional index mutual funds in many ways, including lower costs and improved tax efficiency. However, the benefits of owning ETFs needs to be weighed against any downsides, including the temptation to trade them more than traditional index mutual funds, and any commission charges associated with buying and selling in your brokerage account.

Are ETFs a better investment than traditional index funds? It all depends on how you use them as building blocks for your portfolio. You can either day-trade the SPDR, or you can hold it in your portfolio for the next decade to capture that index's return.

It is all up to you.

Following the evolution of traditional index mutual funds that sprang up as a result of the popularity of Vanguard's first S&P 500 index fund, the financial industry started to expand its offerings beyond the SPDR, introducing ETFs that represent the value, small, small-value, international, and REIT dimensions of the market. Soon to follow were ETFs that represented various countries, international asset classes, sectors, or industries. The financial industry keeps cranking them out, to the point that it is getting a little absurd how many types of exchange-traded index funds are available. To name a few:

Coal	Solar	Leveraged currency
Agriculture commodity	Country rotation	Precious metals
Double long	Health care	Financials
Internet architecture	Regional banks	Pharmaceuticals
Consumer goods	Home construction	Oil & gas exploration
Medical devices	Biotechnology	Natural resources
South Korea	Nuclear energy	Global infrastructure
Clean energy	Green	Cancer
Emerging cancer	Cardio devices	Automotive
Ireland	Grains	Healthcare diagnostic

Stockbrokers and financial advisers are celebrating the smorgasbord of sector ETFs and now suggest that *your* success as an investor relies on *their* ability to mix and match these sector ETFs in just the right way to create a properly diversified portfolio for your long-term financial goals.

But wait a minute! Before you let Wall Street muddle up your portfolio of sector ETFs, it is time to take a giant step backward and reestablish the meaning and purpose of "diversification," especially as it relates to building a common-stock portfolio.

Contrary to Wall Street's self-promoting interests, diversification does NOT mean owning the top ten industries, the top five countries, and the two trendiest ETFs. It means investing in different components of the market that potentially have low correlation in the short run, even though similar returns are expected in the long run.

If there is one thing to remember from this chapter, it is this: Diversification does NOT mean owning the top ten industries, the top five countries, and the two trendiest ETFs. It means investing in different components of the market that have low correlation in the short run, though similar expected returns in the long run.

As we discussed in chapter 4, the easiest way to own a diversified common-stock portfolio is to own the total stock market in one total stock market index fund. Sounds simple enough, and it is.

But let's say you want to take this simple approach one step further and add an extra degree of diversification beyond the total stock market index, which is heavily weighted toward large-cap stocks. How should you proceed? Diversifying a common-stock portfolio beyond a total stock market index fund means first identifying different components of the stock market that might move dissimilarly to each other or have low correlation in the short run, but are likely to have similar returns over the long run.

A good example of this would be dividing up the total stock market into large-company stocks and small-company stocks, and investing in index funds that represent these dimensions of the market. In this instance, the primary goal isn't to "beat the total stock market," with your small-cap addition, it is to capture the return of both dimensions of the market while potentially reducing portfolio volatility. This example can be taken one step further by adding value, international, and REIT index funds to your portfolio mix of common stocks, as discussed in chapter 4.

Wall Street's attempts at beating a benchmark index by identifying sector index funds that represent the top industries and top countries and trendiest fads is as preposterous as its attempts to beat the market with individual stocks or actively managed mutual funds. The same types of market efficiencies found in individual stock selection carry over to sectors, countries, and trendy ETFs. That should come as no surprise, though, because sectors, countries, and trendy ETF's are made up of those same individual stocks.

Reflecting back on the example of Microsoft in chapter 8, the market efficiencies that can cause a complete disconnect between the company's financials and its stock price are the same types of market efficiencies that hold true with industries, countries, and trends.

You might get lucky investing in one trend or two, for one year or two, but to invest in the top industries, countries, and trends in an attempt to outperform a broad market average over the next decade or two is akin more to gambling than to investing. Remember, stock markets around the world are more efficient than you are lucky.

Part of this growing interest in sector, country, and trendy ETFs stems from the fact that our world seems to be reaching an inflection point in the way we allocate our limited resources to meet the growing population's desire for an increased standard of living.

This is causing the dynamics of global capitalism to unfold in extraordinary, unpredictable ways. Some of it is good and some of it isn't, but it is unfolding at a pace that inspires at least one Coffeehouse Investor. As more people around the world are given an opportunity to improve the quality of life for themselves and others through hard work and ingenuity, it accelerates the need for creative minds to come together and form new alliances and new businesses to solve the challenges created by all this change.

As an investor in common stocks, how are you going to invest in the companies that participate in this extraordinary unfolding of ideas and opportunities? Why not let the market efficiencies that are at work in global economies unfold as they should, and invest in all the companies through low-cost, broadly diversified global index funds?

If you think Wall Street has done a good job of cluttering up the good idea of index funds, it gets worse.

The financial industry is now offering us newfangled index funds with a different twist on how the underlying index is constructed, in an effort to beat the market and outperform conventional index funds.

Traditionally, most of the popular indexes, like the S&P 500 index of large-cap stocks or the Russell 2000 index of small-cap stocks, have been constructed using the market capitalization method to determine a company's weight within an index. The makers of these newfangled index funds suggest that the weights should be based not on a company's market capitalization but on other factors, like the earnings of a company or its dividend payout.

The way these funds explain their methodology for an improved index construction and the track record they offer up using simulated historical data are impressive, but are they any better than traditional index funds, especially with the added costs involved? Wall Street certainly thinks so. What else are they going to say?

The irony of sizing up these newfangled index funds compared to traditional index funds is that you will only know which methodology and which index fund come out ahead after one has come out ahead—ten or twenty years from now. The fact that one will inevitably come out ahead doesn't mean it is a better index fund, it just means that the underlying index was constructed differently and that method of construction happened to have a better ten-year run compared to the other index.

As long as you own a broadly diversified, low-cost portfolio of index funds, the ones you choose aren't nearly as important as *sticking with the funds you choose,* especially when other index funds outperform the ones you own.

The explosion in exchange-traded funds and newfangled index funds will continue, because investors' interest in index funds continues. With over one thousand index funds to choose from, how should you sort through all these index funds to find the right ones for your Coffeehouse Investor portfolio? Fortunately for you and me, when it comes to building a common-stock portfolio, the more things change, the more they stay the same. The easiest way to get broad stock market diversification is through ownership of a "total stock market index" fund, and that can be accomplished through either a traditional index mutual fund, a newfangled index fund, or an exchange-traded fund.

If you feel that a total stock market index fund is weighted too heavily toward large-cap domestic companies and you want to diversify beyond that simple approach, ask yourself the question, "Am I adding another fund to diversify my stock market investment, or am I adding another index fund to outperform it?"

Your answer to that question will guide your decision to invest.

There are many ways to build a Coffeehouse Investor portfolio beyond a total stock market index fund, and I have listed a few strategies in chapter 4, but that does not mean that those combinations are the "right" way, because there is no "right" or "wrong" way to build a Coffeehouse Investor portfolio, as long as you are intent on approximating the stock market's return over the next ten years and beyond.

For example, how much small, value, international, emerging market, and REIT exposure should you include to complement your total stock market index fund? Your neighbor will argue that you should have 20 percent, your stockbroker will argue that you should have twice that amount plus a commodities ETF, and you are thinking, why not keep things simple and split it down the middle?

The percentage allocations of various index funds aren't nearly as important as staying true to the allocations you choose, buying and selling them along the way only for rebalancing purposes.

Despite Wall Street's attempts to clutter up the investing landscape with an expanding list of ETFs and newfangled index funds, there are some unique investments that have recently been introduced and are sure to complement many investors' efforts to build wealth, ignore Wall Street, and get on with their lives.

As countries and global economies continue to expand, there is increased interest in investing in international and emerging markets. Traditionally, investors have owned three index funds representing the domestic, international, and emerging markets. Now you can purchase one "all-world" index fund that offers an ideal opportunity to participate in the worldwide markets with one simple index fund.[1]

Although this discussion has centered largely on common stocks, many of these advances in financial products, especially ETFs, have carried over into bond investments as well. Bonds and other fixed-income investments can play an important role in your portfolio, especially as you get older, not only to reduce risk, but also to generate income for you during your retirement years.

Speaking of index funds, bonds, and asset allocation, the financial industry now offers "target" or "lifestyle" funds that consist of a portfolio of low-cost index funds, including an appropriate allocation to a bond index fund. Over time, the fund provider increases the bond allocation to reflect the reduced risk that is generally appropriate for a decreasing time horizon.

For instance, if you are twenty-five years old, you might invest in Vanguard's Target Retirement 2045 fund, which assumes you will retire around the year 2045. If you are fifty-five years old, Vanguard's Target Retirement 2020 fund would be more appropriate for you, assuming the year 2020 approximates your retirement date.

Despite the incredible growth of financial products surrounding the simple concept of indexing, the three Coffeehouse Investor principles haven't changed a bit. In fact, with Wall Street trying to complicate the simple concept of indexing, the three Coffeehouse principles are more important than ever before.

11 LET'S HAVE SOME FUN

THERE IS NO WAY I WOULD EVER DRAG MYSELF OUT of bed at 5:45 on Saturday mornings for a twenty-minute walk in the dark and the cold rain to meet up with five friends at a corner coffeehouse table if I didn't think it was going to be a ton of fun.

But it is.

Every time.

With all that life throws our way, we need to take advantage of the fun times—making sure our fun times accentuate our daily experiences as well as our lifetime goals.

And for most of us who are serious about building wealth, ignoring Wall Street, and getting on with our lives, I sus-

pect the importance of making the right investment decisions today precedes any great desire to have fun in the
stock market. But for some (including me), somewhere
deep inside our psyche is a part that wants to whoop it
up—you know, get a little more involved in this stock
market thing than simply indexing our stock investments
and getting on with our lives.

I learned all about having fun in the stock market during
my stockbroker days many years ago, from a client I
stumbled upon while cold-calling from the yellow pages.

The conversations that evolve from talking to complete
strangers who would rather not talk to you are rather
interesting, and when you ask that person on the other
end of the line to take a chance on your next hot stock
idea, it takes a lot of quick talking to get past "hello."
But one time, a deep, heavily accented voice caught me
by surprise and took me up on my offer. After he
bought my hot stock idea, we watched it go up and up.
It was pretty neat to see my hot stock idea go up and
up, because with each successive phone call I had a
sense this person was thinking I was a pretty hot stock
picker. The more I think he thinks I'm a pretty hot
stock picker the more I believe it, and before long I
think therefore I am.

The exciting part about being a pretty hot stock picker is
that the new client gives you a chance to pick another hot

stock, and gosh, this stock doesn't just go up, it also goes down. One day this client decided to change the subject from stock market things and invited me to climb a mountain.

I thought to myself, I don't want to climb a mountain; maybe I could get this guy to caddie for me instead.

But my client was persistent, and one month later, on a Saturday morning, I was halfway up a glacier on the side of a mountain in northern California.

Cold, hungry, and thirsty.

After making it to the top of that miserable thing, I vowed never to climb another mountain in my life. Unfortunately, things don't always go as planned, because back at my desk in Seattle a big white thing called Mount Rainier kept smiling at me.

Yeah, yeah, yeah.

A couple of months later, while coughing, shaking, and shivering on top of Rainier, I vowed again to never climb another mountain. A few mountains later I stopped making those vows, because vows just get you in trouble anyway.

Climbing a mountain has little to do with hanging by a thread hooked to a ledge near the side of a cliff. Climbing a mountain has a lot to do with putting one foot in front of the other, slowly and methodically, even when you don't feel like it, until there's only one way to go—down, because you have reached the top.

After noticing I had mastered the art of putting one foot in front of the other much better than I had mastered the art of picking stocks, my persistent client called and said, "Let's climb Mount McKinley!"

What?

Climb the tallest mountain in North America? Climb one of the coldest mountains in the world? Climb the mountain they call Denali that killed twenty people in the previous three years? Forget it. Think golf balls.

Six months later I discovered that the major difference between climbing Denali and climbing Rainier was the thickness of one's underwear and the thinness of one's patience with that person one is stuck with in a tent for three weeks.

You will notice that the more I talk about my mountain-climbing prowess the less I talk about my stock-picking prowess, because while I was climbing up the mountains my client's stocks were going down the tubes.

One day I asked this client of mine why he continued to invest in my stock ideas with the same devil-may-care attitude with which he climbed mountains. He replied matter-of-factly, "It's fun!"

Hmm, okay. So maybe you just wanna have fun.

If you want to have fun in the stock market there is one simple rule to follow: Make sure you—not some mutual fund manager—is the one having fun. When you turn your money over to a mutual fund manager in pursuit of a little fun and excitement in the stock market, you are defeating your purpose. The mutual fund manager ends up being the one having fun—at your expense—and you give up any realistic chance of beating the stock market over the long term.

How boring—and how dumb.

But what the heck, let's see what happens when we do turn our money over to a mutual fund manager in pursuit of a little fun. Let's invest $500 a month for twenty years in the average actively managed mutual fund (which, incidentally, underperformed the stock market average by 16 percent annually over the five-year period ending 1997) and compare it to an investment in an unmanaged index fund that mirrors the Wilshire 5000 index.

At the end of five years, your actively managed mutual fund is trailing the index fund by $3,320.

Are you having fun yet?

At the end of ten years, your actively managed mutual fund is trailing the index fund by $18,175.

Are you having fun yet?

At the end of fifteen years, your actively managed mutual fund is trailing the index fund by $56,916.

Are you having fun yet?

At the end of twenty years you are now ready to retire, and your actively managed fund is trailing the indexed portfolio by $142,549.

Are you ha—

Oh, forget it.

The point is, if you are making a million dollars a year and at the end of the year are getting paid million-dollar bonuses, like the presidents and CEOs of most financial institutions, I guess you are entitled to have a little fun in the stock market.

But when you are getting up each morning and struggling to get your children to school on time so you can make it to work on time and trying to figure out how you can make it to two different soccer games that night—and you are doing all you can to save and invest $500 a month in your 401(k) and trying to find another $500 a month to put in a college education fund for your little soccer stars, and you know that if managed mutual funds continue to underperform the stock market average as they have in the past it could cost you hundreds of thousands of dollars at retirement—

uh, maybe we should take our fun elsewhere.

If you want to have some fun in the stock market, the solution is not to turn your money over to some mutual fund manager. The solution is to first index the majority of your stock market assets to make sure most of your money is at least keeping up with the stock market average and then take a small portion of your stock market money and invest it in your own common stock ideas . . . and have the time of your life!

There are many reasons why you might want to take a little detour on this journey and invest in individual common stocks. Some of us (including me) love to gamble, and I suspect that the rush of adrenaline one gets when placing a chip on red is not unlike buying a hot stock that makes widgets and gizmos and then watching it go from two to twenty and back down to two again (after we've sold it at nineteen and five eighths, of course).

Yet the more I ponder the possibility of a correlation between investing and gambling, the more I am inclined to think there is a stronger force than gambling luring so many investors to pick individual stocks. This force is a fundamental desire to compete. After all, the strength of our country is built on the freedom to compete and win, compete and lose, pick yourself up and compete again. I love to compete as much as anyone, whether it's in business or basketball, and I have found that the best way to pass the time during a five-day snowstorm is to play a little poker in the tent.

But the main reason I enjoy picking my own individual stocks with a small portion of my total portfolio is that I want to be part of a particular company that has a successful product or service that has evolved over time from an explosion of bright ideas.

All we have to do is look around us to see this explosion of ideas unfolding before our eyes. I am reminded of this explosion of ideas every time I sit down to do some work on my personal computer, because next to my personal computer, which has a word processor attached to a spreadsheet program attached to a database management program hooked up to a LaserJet printer, is my 1923 Underwood typewriter. I doubt there has ever been a time, a place, or a country that has provided such a dynamic opportunity as ours has for creative human beings to take a 1923 Underwood typewriter idea and sketch it and mold it and alter it and transform it into something called a technology revolution.

Ideas that arise from our essential creativity—they just keep coming, one after the other, and the ideas of yesterday that are obsolete today barely have time to get out of the way for the better ideas that are germinating today and will be ready to go tomorrow.

Even though this investment journey has shown us that the best way to build a successful common-stock portfolio is to forgo investing in individual companies in favor of investing in our country's collective creativity, this journey wouldn't be complete if we didn't address that part of our emotions that enjoys the challenge of investing in the great ideas and great products of individual companies.

This doesn't mean we need to become "stock market junkies" who are completely caught up in the workings of the stock market and subscribe to newsletters, read mutual fund magazines, attend financial seminars, watch financial television shows, trade on the Internet, and calculate account values daily. This part of the journey is for investors who realize the importance of approximating the stock market average with the majority of their stock market investments but still want to try their hand at buying a few stocks here and there because after all, it can be fun and challenging to pit your wits against everyone else in the stock market. And who knows? Somewhere among the millions and millions of stock pickers might be the next Warren Buffett.

But I'm not sure it's worth risking your entire portfolio to find out you aren't.

The important thing to remember when pitting your wits against everyone else is to keep your emotions of fear and greed in check so that your stock market fun remains fun, because when fear and greed aren't controlled, buying and selling individual stocks can quickly become a miserable experience.

Let's look at a few ways you can fulfill the need to have fun in the stock market without allowing it to adversely impact your overall stock market portfolio.

- Pick stocks, not mutual funds, and pick them yourself. If you pick mutual funds, you allow a mutual fund manager to pick stocks for you, which defeats the purpose of having fun in the first place.

- Start by investing no more than 5 percent to 15 percent of your total portfolio in stocks. A larger commitment than this could significantly impact your total investment return.
- At year-end, compare the return of your stocks with the return of the stock market average. Either this comparison will give you an appreciation for the difficulty of outperforming the stock market averages, or it will give you a chance to brag about your stock-picking prowess.

When looking for stocks to buy, it helps to remember that a stock is much more than a three-letter symbol in *The Wall Street Journal*. It is a share of a company, with a headquarters made up of people who get up in the mornings and put in a hard day's work to make that company successful.

With that in mind, it's a good idea to invest in companies you know and understand. For instance, if you have first-hand knowledge that a company's employees not only enjoy working at the company but provide a service or product that is in continual demand, chances are you are going to be much more successful investing in the common stock of that company than you would owning a no-name company halfway across the country that you are unfamiliar with.

For example, if I were to buy into a company with my fun money, I might choose Nordstrom, because I appreciate its commitment to customer service, and I know for a fact that customer service keeps Nordstrom's clients coming back. I might buy Microsoft, because I have edited this book what seems like six thousand times on Microsoft software, and for some reason I like a company whose product helps me transform my dreams and ideas into realities. I might buy Boeing, because I like the way its employees listen to their customers and build airplanes to fit the needs of the airline industry.

For me, the important thing in owning Nordstrom, Microsoft, and Boeing is not to get caught up in all the stuff Wall Street gets caught up in, because if I get caught up in Wall Street stuff, like fifty-two-week highs and lows, price-earnings ratios, and long-term debt, I am likely to underperform the stock market average the way mutual fund managers do. The problem with putting these three companies under a microscope and analyzing all the fifty-two-week-long-term-price-earnings-book-to-ratio stuff, like Wall Street does, is that you tend to lose sight of the fact that these companies have great products, great customer service, and, most importantly, great people.

I mean, who really cares if Nordstrom is expanding too fast, Boeing is having temporary production problems, and Microsoft is knocking heads with the Fed. If companies that have great products, great customer service, and great people continue to grow their products and accentuate their customer service by embracing the great ideas of their employees and customers, more often than not they will be around another twenty-five years and their success will eventually be reflected in my portfolio.

For the most part, it makes sense to invest in companies you can easily understand. It doesn't take a rocket scientist to understand the necessity of Boeing airplanes (no offense to all the great rocket scientists at Boeing), Nordstrom's attention to detail, or the usefulness of Microsoft software.

On the flip side, in my neighborhood is headquartered a biotech company with a crazy name like Bioenzymintrixnex, Inc., or something. I don't follow this company; in fact, I haven't a clue what it does, and with a name like that I'm not sure I want to find out, but I do know it has never turned a profit, and I don't know if it ever will.

When it comes to picking a stock for the fun portion of my portfolio, this company is not for me. But that is not to say this isn't a great investment, because maybe you are the type of investor who is willing to take time to visit the headquarters and talk with the employees to learn more about their company, and maybe after learning about it you decide that even though it is not making any money today, this company has a great product or idea and is worth the risk.

In this situation, the chance of your losing some or all of your money is much greater than the chance of my losing some or all of my money in Nordstrom, Microsoft, or Boeing.

That's the downside.

However, this biotech company might enter into a joint venture next month with an international conglomerate that takes its product or idea and markets it all over the world, and your initial investment might end up going up 1,000 percent next week. That's the upside.

Isn't all this upside/downside stuff fun?

Once you buy a company you like, that's when the real fun begins. Anybody can buy a stock. It's the decision of whether and when to sell it that gets a little hairy. Don't you just love those stories heard down at the neighborhood coffeehouse about Uncle Joe's great-aunt's nephew's first cousin's neighbor's wife, who bought shares of Procter & Gamble ninety-three years ago and still owns the same shares, which over the years have grown and multiplied like jackrabbits and are now worth more than a million jackrabbits? If you never hold onto a stock long enough to let that "through-the-roof" stock go through the next roof and the roof after that, you give up the opportunity to be the topic of discussion at some future neighborhood coffeehouse because your desire to book a profit caused you to sell too early.

The sell decision on a "through-the-roof" stock is complicated because you will kick yourself if you sell and it continues to go through three more roofs, but you will kick yourself harder if you don't sell and it proceeds to drop through the floor.

The decision whether and when to sell a stock that drops through the floor is a little more emotional, because it implies we made a mistake in deciding to buy the stock in the first place, and sometimes it is hard for us to admit we made a mistake. But heck, having the courage to admit we made a mistake is half the fun of picking our own stocks, because it makes those through-the-roof discoveries so much sweeter. Once you do sell, it frees you up to take that money and look for another through-the-roof stock.

When evaluating whether or not to sell a stock, it helps to make the decision in the context of what the stock market did during the time period you owned the stock. If your common stock is down 20 percent during a five-month period but the stock market average is down 15 percent during the same five-month period, a decision to sell the stock and cut your losses may be a bit premature, because your stock hasn't been a complete disaster compared to the stock market average.

If you begin to notice that all your buy decisions should have been sells and all your sell decisions should have been buys, and you start to get frustrated, remember—the goal is to have fun.

12 THE JOURNEY CONTINUES

WE ARE TRAVELING TOGETHER ON THIS PLANET IN THE middle of an infinite universe, trying to stay linked to our families, our communities, and ourselves in a way that brings meaning to our lives.

This journey is a little different for each of us, but in the end, most of us would probably agree that it is the connection to other people in our lives that matters most of all.

That is the purpose of *The New Coffeehouse Investor*—to help you get on with your life by introducing three simple principles that will guide you in building financial and *emotional* wealth. But creating wealth for a secure future is easier said than done, especially when there are so many pressures to spend it today.

Speaking of spending it, there seems to be a lot written these days about the financial decay of our society, how we are becoming a nation of spenders, running up the credit card bills and running down our savings accounts.

But along with the woeful tales of those who spend too much is another story that needs to be told: that of millions of Americans who *do* want to take responsibility for their saving and investing decisions by making the right choices today for a secure financial future tomorrow.

The challenge of wanting to take personal responsibility for our financial well-being is that our choices are so ill defined and results so uncertain that we hardly know where to start. To complicate things, we are bombarded by Wall Street's relentless advertisements suggesting that our investment success lies in its hands, or at least in its ability to pick stocks and mutual funds.

Eventually, we start thinking that our responsibility becomes Wall Street's responsibility. Instead of focusing on our saving and spending, we start focusing on stocks and mutual funds. It is hard enough achieving clarity of purpose with our own saving and spending issues; why complicate things by pursuing the top stocks and mutual funds, an endeavor that is irrelevant to your financial success?

The goal of saving enough money, investing it in an intelligent manner, and then spending it wisely during retirement can seem overwhelming. It doesn't have to be. For those of you who are committed to taking responsibility for your financial future, a good place to begin your journey is by embracing three lifelong principles that are in your control. That is what *The New Coffeehouse Investor* is all about.

1. Don't put all your eggs in one basket.

The key to building a successful portfolio is to diversify your assets in such a way that you maximize your chances of reaching your financial goals with a minimum amount of risk.

2. There is no such thing as a free lunch.

Because markets are efficient, any attempt to beat the market is likely to prove disastrous to your long-term financial health. Thus, it is essential that you capture the entire return of each asset class, a goal easily accomplished through low-cost index funds, and leave it at that.

3. Save for a rainy day.

Developing a long-term financial plan, with a keen eye on your saving and spending levels, is essential for you to reach your long-term goals.

These principles are important stuff, because we have entered a new era of investing, one that literally demands you modify your perception of what building long-term wealth is all about. This era ushers out the excesses of the past twenty-five years, brought on by an overheated stock market and real estate market, and ushers in an era of personal responsibility. This new era will consist of reduced returns in the markets and increased opportunities in your life. It is an era that will necessitate that you embrace a successful investment philosophy and then stick with it in good times and bad. It is an era that will require you to turn away from the frustrating fluctuations of your investments and tune in to your passions for this world.

Sometimes I think one of the reasons I have been so relentless in advancing the Coffeehouse Investor principles is that I am energized by connecting with people who *are* tuned in to their passions and getting on with their lives. They inspire me to do the same.

These are the people who realize that fulfillment in life comes not from the size of a bank account but from the amount of energy put forth pursuing things that give meaning to their existence.

These are the people who have established a few *lifetime* principles that are essential to building emotional and financial wealth, and that is what I want to leave you with as our journey through life continues.

Tune in to yourself. Call it what you want—intuition, commonsense smarts, a gut feeling—one thing is certain: You know more than you think you know. Have a little confidence in what your heart tells you to be true, and go with it. Inside of you is a creative spark that yearns to be fueled by a recognition of your talents and gifts. It might take you ten days to fuel that spark, or it might take ten years, but it is worth lighting that fire within.

Take it from someone who learned this the hard way: Nothing is worse than wasting your life away at something that leaves you unfulfilled. On the flip side, I have also found that nothing is more gratifying than waking up each morning with a zeal for your work, immersing yourself in a family, career, or community that allows you to share your essential creativity with the world.

You don't have to be a Nobel Laureate to change the world. You do have to discover your spark of creativity to transform your neighborhood—the world you live in. In doing so, you will be given opportunities to make a positive difference every day of your life. Don't pass them up. The world needs you now more than ever before.

Tune in to your friends. Stop, look, and listen to those people who inspire you, who will help fuel your fire of creativity as you pursue your dreams and careers. These are the ones who lift you up and spur you on when you are facing your fears and dealing with the inevitable disappointments along the way. Someday you will look back and realize that these were the treasured ones who allowed you to ignite that spark and become your true self. But be careful of becoming self-absorbed in your pursuits. For friendships to be sustained, you had best reciprocate the same thoughtful presence in return. Take time along the way to acknowledge these people, and let your thanks be your offer of the same encouragement to others in the world.

Tune in to your community. It is the energy of the universe. Some people call it God; others refer to it as a spirituality, and still others a life force. However you define it, a wonderful energy evolves when we come together in community to enact positive change in this world. This thing called community might take the form of your workplace environment, your church group affiliation, or your weekly golfing buddies. Whatever the relationship might be, this connection is integral to discovering your essential creativity and living a rich life. Step up, step out, and get involved; the world is screaming for your creative energies to surface, and the time to start is now.

In stepping out you are going to encounter problems—*big* problems—along the way. Big deal. Problems create new ideas and new opportunities and new businesses. One example of this is the way we are beginning to apply our unlimited people resources to deal with our limited natural resources, and this only addresses our United States of America. These same opportunities exist around the globe as people work toward improving the quality of their own lives and the lives of those around them.

The way I see it, we don't have any other choice. It is a matter of survival, and that is why I am so optimistic. When we are forced to find solutions, we usually do, even though we might be a little slow on the uptake. That is just the way we operate.

What does all this have to do with your life now, your retirement sometime in the future, and *The New Coffeehouse Investor*? Everything, if you want to be an active participant in this unfolding of life. This economic dynamism is going to create wonderful opportunities, from both a personal-involvement and an investment standpoint. If you want to join in, it will require that you unclutter and simplify your life so that your essential creativity can rise to the surface in ways that meet the needs of the world.

The challenge of building wealth, ignoring Wall Street, and getting on with our lives can appear intimidating and insurmountable. It doesn't have to be. When we unclutter one part of our life, we enrich another part, and that is what this investment journey is all about. When we simplify investing, we take another step toward discovering our contagious spirit and our unique energy in such a way that we impact our world, making this a better place for everyone. I suspect that is what most of us would say life is all about.

I wish you the best of luck.

APPENDIX

The following table is a partial list of index funds, divided into categories. Included in this list are exchange-traded funds (ETFs)—index funds that trade on stock exchanges and can be bought and sold in the same manner as individual stocks. For more information, please refer to the following Web sites:

www.dfaus.com
www.etfzone.com
www.ishares.com
www.morningstar.com
www.vanguard.com

CATEGORY	SYMBOL
TOTAL WORLD INDEX FUNDS	
ISHARES MSCI ACWI INDEX ETF	ACWI
VANGUARD TOTAL WORLD INDEX FUND	VTWSX
VANGUARD TOTAL WORLD INDEX ETF	VT
TOTAL STOCK MARKET INDEX FUNDS (DOMESTIC)	
ISHARES R3000 ETF	IWV
VANGUARD TOTAL ST. MKT	VTSMX
LARGE-CAP INDEX FUNDS	
DOMINI SOCIAL EQUITY	DSEFX
ISHARES S&P 500 ETF	IVV
S&P DEP. RCPT. (SPIDER) ETF	SPY
VANGUARD INDEX 500	VFINX
VANGUARD LARGE CAP ETF	W
SMALL-CAP INDEX FUNDS	
DFA U.S. MICRO CAP	DFSCX
ISHARES SP 600 ETF	IJR
VANGUARD SMALL CAP	NAESX
LARGE-VALUE INDEX FUNDS	
DFA U.S. LARGE CAP VALUE	DFLVX
ISHARES R1000 VALUE ETF	IWD
VANGUARD VALUE	VIVAX
VANGUARD VALUE ETF ETF	VTV
SMALL-VALUE INDEX FUNDS	
DFA U.S. SMALL VALUE	DFSVX
ISHARES SP 600 VALUE ETF	IJS
VANGUARD SM. VALUE	VISVX
VANGUARD SM. VALUE ETF	VBR
INTERNATIONAL INDEX FUNDS	
ISHARES MSCI EAFE ETF	EFA
DFA INT'L VALUE	EFIVX
DFA INT'L SMALL VALUE	DISVX
DFA INT'L CORE EQUITY	DFIEX
VANGUARD TOTAL INT'L	VGTSX
EMERGING-MARKETS INDEX FUNDS	
VANGUARD EMERGING MARKETS ETF	VWO
VANGUARD EMERGING MARKETS FUND	VEIEX
DFA EMERGING MARKETS CORE	DFCEX

CATEGORY	SYMBOL
REAL ESTATE INVESTMENT TRUST (REITS)	
ISHARES DOW JONES REIT	IYR
DFA REIT	DFREX
VANGUARD REIT	VGSIX
BOND FUNDS	
ISHARES LEHMAN AGGREGATE ETF	AGG
ISHARES GOLDMAN SACHS CORP. ETF	LQD
ISHARES LEHMAN TIPS ETF	TIP
VANGUARD SHORT TERM BOND	VBISX
VANGUARD INTERMEDIATE BOND	VBIIX
VANGUARD TOTAL BOND	VBMFX
VANGUARD SHORT TERM BOND ETF	BSV
VANGUARD INTERMEDIATE BOND ETF	BIV
VANGUARD TOTAL BOND ETF	BND

BONDS

You can invest in either bonds or bond funds. Although they have similar features, these two investments can potentially have strikingly different results. Bonds have a stated maturity, when the face value of the bond is redeemed and returned to the investor. Bond funds, on the other hand, don't have a stated maturity. Consequently, if interest rates rise due to a stronger economy, your bond fund will decline in value, and it might be a long, long time before interest rates decline enough for the value of your bond fund to return to 100 percent of your original investment.

For that reason, the best bond funds to own are short- and intermediate-term indexed bond funds, because the fees are so low. We discovered in chapter 6 that expenses on stock mutual funds can significantly impact the total return over time. When it comes to investing in bond funds, fees are even more important because they generally eat up a greater percentage of your annual income.

For investors who want to invest in U.S. Treasury securities, check the following Web site for a step-by-step guide to buying them, current auction information, and downloadable forms: www.publicdebt.treas.gov.

NOTES

PREFACE

1. *The American Heritage Dictionary* (Boston: Houghton Mifflin Co., 1976).
2. Earnings and Employment 1997. U.S. Department of Labor, Bureau of Labor Statistics.

CHAPTER 1: THE COFFEEHOUSE INVESTOR

1. Thomas J. Stanley and William D. Danko, *The Millionaire Next Door* (Atlanta: Longstreet Press, 1996).

CHAPTER 2: THIS THING CALLED RISK

1. 1971–2008.

CHAPTER 3: APPROXIMATING THE STOCK MARKET AVERAGE

1. 2008 Morningstar.
2. Based on personal interviews conducted by the author.
3. Domestic large-cap mutual funds as of June 30, 2008. 2008 Morningstar.

CHAPTER 5: MY FAVORITE PIECE OF PIE

1. 2008 Morningstar.
2. 2008 Morningstar.

CHAPTER 7: LIFE, LOGIC, AND PARADOXES

1. *The American Heritage Dictionary* (Boston, MA: Houghton Mifflin Co., 1976).
2. 2008 Morningstar.
3. 2008 Morningstar.
4. *American Heritage Dictionary.*

CHAPTER 8: TRAVELS OF A COFFEEHOUSE INVESTOR

1. According to the DALBAR, Inc. 2008 Quantitative Analysis of Investor Behavior, over the twenty-year period ending December 31, 2007, the average equity mutual fund investor held his fund just over three years and earned an annualized return of 4.48 percent, underperforming the S&P 500 index by more than 7 percent. Used with permission.
2. Based on data provided by Legg Mason. January 1, 2006, to June 30, 2008.

CHAPTER 9: SPENDING IT

1. Some of the more popular financial planning tools can be found at www.fidelity.com, www.vanguard.com, and www .analyzenow.com.

CHAPTER 10: INDEX FUNDS AND BEYOND

1. See the appendix for a listing of "total world" ETFs.

ADDITIONAL READING

Bernstein, William J. *The Four Pillars of Investing: Lessons for Building a Winning Portfolio.* New York: McGraw-Hill, 2002.

Bogle, John. *Bogle on Mutual Funds: New Perspectives for the Intelligent Investor.* Burr Ridge, IL: Irwin Professional Publishing, 1993.

Farrell, Paul B. *The Lazy Person's Guide to Investing.* New York: Warner Business Books, 2004.

Ferri, Richard. *The ETF Book—All You Need to Know About Exchange Traded Funds.* Hoboken, NJ: John Wiley & Sons, Inc., 2007.

Hazan, Marcella. *Essentials of Classic Italian Cooking.* New York: Alfred A. Knopf, Inc., 1992.

Hogan, Ben, and Herbert W. Wind. *Ben Hogan's Five Lessons: The Modern Fundamentals of Golf.* Trumbull, CT: Golf Digest, 1985.

Lindbergh, Anne M. *Gift From the Sea.* New York: Pantheon Books, 1991.

Malkiel, Burton. *A Random Walk Down Wall Street: Including a Lifecycle Guide to Personal Investing.* New York: W. W. Norton & Company, Inc., 1995.

Moore, Thomas. *Dark Nights of the Soul: A Guide to Finding Your Way Through Life's Ordeals.* New York: Gotham Books, 2004.

Swedroe, Larry. *The Only Guide to a Winning Investment Strategy You'll Ever Need.* New York: St. Martin's Press, 2005.

Waterman, Jonathan. *Surviving Denali: A Study of Accidents on Mount McKinley, 1903–1990.* Golden, CO: American Alpine Club, 1991.

INDEX

ABOUT THE AUTHOR

Bill Schultheis brings his simple, inspirational message to individual investors and corporate retirement plans as an investment adviser with Soundmark Wealth Management, LLC (a fee-only registered investment adviser), located in Kirkland, Washington. Prior to creating *The Coffeehouse Investor*, he spent thirteen years providing investment advice to individuals, trusts, and institutional accounts for Smith Barney in Seattle, Washington.

To subscribe to the free *Coffeehouse Investor* newsletter, and for more information on Soundmark Wealth Management, LLC, please visit the following Web sites:

www.coffeehouseinvestor.com
www.soundmarkwealth.com

Bill can be reached at billschultheis@yahoo.com.